We Are the Ones
We Have Been Waiting For

We Are the Ones
We Have Been Waiting For

Inner Light in a Time of Darkness

MEDITATIONS

Alice Walker

NEW YORK • LONDON

© 2006 by Alice Walker
All rights reserved.
No part of this book may be reproduced,
in any form, without written permission from the publisher.

Requests for permission to reproduce selections
from this book should be mailed to:
Permissions Department, The New Press,
38 Greene Street, New York, NY 10013.

Published in the United States by
The New Press, New York, 2006
Distributed by W. W. Norton & Company, Inc., New York

LIBRARY OF CONGRESS CATALOGING-IN-PUBLICATION DATA
Walker, Alice, 1944-
We are the ones we have been waiting for :
inner light in a time of darkness / Alice Walker.
     p.   cm.
ISBN-13: 978-1-59558-137-2 (hc)
ISBN-10: 1-59558-137-5 (hc)
I. Title.
PS3573.A425W43 2006
811'.54—dc22   2006013981

The New Press was established in 1990 as a not-for-profit alternative to the large, commercial publishing houses currently
dominating the book publishing industry. The New Press op-
erates in the public interest rather than for private gain, and is
committed to publishing, in innovative ways, works of educa-
tional, cultural, and community value that are often deemed
insufficiently profitable.

www.thenewpress.com

Book design by Kelly Too
Composition by dix!
This book was set in Sabon

Printed in the United States of America

4   6   8   10   9   7   5   3

*To Scott Sanders, Stephen Bray,
and Gary Griffin
With more gratitude and love than you can
probably imagine. You are the men the ancestors
and I were waiting for. Congratulations.*

*and for Amy Goodman, Bernice Johnson
Reagon, and Ayi Kwei Armah
in recognition
and to the Young everywhere
who are standing up*

IF WE ARE TRUE TO HER, THE GODDESS WILL COME TO US. FINDING THE PATH IN ALL DIRECTIONS.

And what will join this standing up and the ones who stood without sweet company will sing and sing back into the mountains and if necessary even under the sea

We are the ones we have been waiting for
—from "Poem for South African Women"
by June Jordan

It was the best of times, it was the worst of times. It was the age of wisdom, it was the age of foolishness. It was the epoch of belief, it was the epoch of incredulity. It was the season of light, it was the season of darkness.

—Charles Dickens, *A Tale of Two Cities*

Contents

Acknowledgments

I wish to thank Diane Wachtell of The New Press for her warm acceptance of *We Are the Ones We Have Been Waiting For: Inner Light in a Time of Darkness*. I am likewise indebted to Ina Howard for her thoughtful comments and editing expertise. Her sensitivity to the tone of the book has helped the creation of its present form.

It is a joy to thank my agent of many years, Wendy Weil, for finding just the right publishing house for a book that contemplates, on a deep, often intimate level, the spiritual trials and practical requirements of this quite alarming period we are living in. I thank my beautiful family of origin simply for Being; for teaching me each day that I was never as lost from my "place" as auntie and elder as I imagined. This is a precious gift for this part of my journey. I would not have missed it for anything.

I thank William Poy Lee for being a powerful ally and friend, whose Capricorn/Tiger instincts quite often save the day.

I thank my parents for loving me beyond my ability to comprehend what they had already lived through by the time I arrived. I thank my grandparents for unconditional love and no reprimands whatsoever.

I thank the community into which I was born for its beauty and simplicity; and the community that continues to nurture me—sangha, circle, women's council—in which I now live.

Namasté.

We Are the Ones
We Have Been Waiting For

Introduction

We Are the Ones We Have Been Waiting For

It is the worst of times. It is the best of times. Try as I might I cannot find a more appropriate opening for this volume: it helps tremendously that these words have been spoken before and, thanks to Charles Dickens, written at the beginning of *A Tale of Two Cities*. Perhaps they have been spoken, written, thought, an endless number of times throughout human history. It is the worst of times because it feels as though the very Earth is being stolen from us, *by us*: the land and air poisoned, the water polluted, the animals disappeared, humans degraded and misguided. War is everywhere. It is the best of times because we have entered a period, if we can bring ourselves to pay attention, of great clarity as to cause and effect. A blessing when we consider how much suffering human beings have endured, in previous millennia, without a clue to its cause. Gods and Goddesses were no doubt created to fill this gap. Because we can now see into every crevice of the globe and because we are free to explore previously unexplored crevices in our own hearts and minds, it is inevitable that everything we have needed to comprehend in order to survive, everything we have needed to understand in the most basic of ways, will be illuminated now. We have only to open our eyes, and awaken to our predicament. We see that we are, alas, a huge part of our problem. However: *We live in a time of global enlightenment.* This alone should make us shout for joy.

It is as if ancient graves, hidden deep in the shadows of the psyche and the earth, are breaking open of their own accord. Unwilling to be silent any longer. Incapable of silence. No leader or people of any country will be safe from these upheavals that lead to exposure, no matter how much the news is managed or how long people's grievances have been kept quiet. Human beings may well be unable to break free of the dictatorship of greed that spreads like a miasma over the world, but no longer will we be an inarticulate and ignorant humanity, confused by our enslavement to superior cruelty and weaponry. We will know at least a bit of the truth about what is going on, and that will set us free. Perhaps not free in the old way of thinking about freedom, as literal escape from enslavement in its various forms, but free in our understanding that our domination is not a comment on our worth. It is an awesome era in which to live.

It was the poet June Jordan who wrote "We are the ones we have been waiting for." Sweet Honey in the Rock turned those words into a song. Hearing this song, I have witnessed thousands of people rise to their feet in joyful recognition and affirmation. We are the ones we've been waiting for because we are able to see what is happening with a much greater awareness than our parents or grandparents, our ancestors, could see. This does not mean we believe, having seen the greater truth of how all oppression is connected, how pervasive and unrelenting, that we can "fix" things. But some of us are not content to have a gap in opportunity and income that drives a wedge between rich and poor, causing the rich to become ever more callous and complacent and the poor to become ever more wretched and humiliated. Not willing to ignore starving and brutalized children. Not willing to let women be stoned or mutilated without protest. Not willing to stand quietly by as farmers are destroyed by people who have never farmed, and plants are engineered to self-destruct. Not willing to disappear into our flower gardens, Mercedes Benzes or sylvan lawns. We have wanted all our lives to know that Earth, who has somehow obtained human beings as her custodians, was also capable of creating humans who could minister to her needs, and the needs of her creation. *We are the ones*.

June Jordan, who died of cancer in 2002, was a brilliant, fierce, radical, and frequently furious poet. We were friends for thirty years. Not once in that time did she step back from what was transpiring politically and morally in the world. She spoke up, and led her students, whom she adored, to do the same.

We were not friends who saw each other often; not the kind of friends who discussed unpublished work. In fact, we sometimes disagreed profoundly with each other. We were the kind of friends, instead, who understood that we were forever on the same side: the side of the poor, the economically, spiritually and politically oppressed, "the wretched of the earth." And on the side, too, of the revolutionaries, teachers and spiritual leaders who seek transformation of the world. That any argument arising between us would be silenced as we turned our combined energy to scrutinize an oncoming foe. I took great comfort in this reality. It seems a model of what can help us rebalance the world. Friendship with others: populations, peoples, countries, that is, in a sense, impersonal.

Many people are already working on this model. They are the ones who go to places like Afghanistan and Iraq and place their bodies between the bombs of the United States and the infrastructure of the local water supply. They are the ones who collect food and medicine for those deprived. The ones who monitor the war(s) and report news that would not otherwise be heard. They are the ones who feel no joy at another's defeat. No satisfaction at another's pain.

In fact, the happiness that imbues this kind of friendship, whether for an individual or a country, or an act, is like an inner light, a compass we might steer by as we set out across the lengthening darkness. It comes from the simple belief and understanding that what one is feeling and doing is right. That it is right to protect rather than terrorize others; right to feed people rather than withhold food and medicine; right to want the freedom and joyful existence of all humankind. Right to want this freedom and joy for all creatures that exist already, or that might come into existence. *Existence, we are now learning, is not finished!* It is a happiness that comes from honoring the peace or the possibility of peace that lives within one's own heart. A deep knowing that we are the Earth—our separation from Earth perhaps our greatest illusion—and that we stand, with gratitude and love, by our planetary Self.

When you read this book you may not be surprised that many of its "meditations" were delivered as talks. There is a reason for this. Perhaps you already know that many writers write because they secretly believe they cannot talk, or they don't like to talk, or they feel they have nothing to say. This describes this writer more often than not, in any case. Or did describe me until a year or so ago.

Until that time, whenever I accepted an invitation to speak—to a college or high school graduating class, an association of yoga teachers, a gathering of Buddhists—I sat down and wrote what I wished to say, frankly worrying that if I did not write it down I would forget it, memory of the non-fictional not being a strength. One of these pieces has since become a small book: a talk to midwives that I gave shortly after 9/11: *Sent By Earth: A Message from the Grandmother Spirit*, another a CD: *Orchids; What It Means to Be Black*, which was delivered at a gathering of Black yoga teachers. The talk that I gave some years ago at UC Santa Cruz commemorating Martin Luther King's birthday and publicly affirming my grief over his assassination, "How It Feels to Know Somebody Died for You: Living With the Voice of the Beloved," is sometimes played, in celebration of his life, on radio.

I have been cured of my dependence on a script, however. It happened in the following way: I was invited to visit South Korea by a Korean priestess who failed to inform me until we arrived in Seoul that I was expected to deliver nine lectures in two different cities in six days. They were each to be two hours long. This was of course humanly impossible, at least for this human. After explaining that I would never attempt to talk to any stranger for more than an hour, but that I would entertain questions from the audience after each talk, we set out on the most grueling tour of my life. In addition to the lectures, the Korean priestess and I had written a book together (about Women and God and Life) that became a bestseller in Seoul, and there were print and other media interviews practically non-stop. I returned from South Korea seriously depleted. But I gained important self-knowledge: when faced with thousands of people who spoke English, if at all, as a second language, I could talk for at least an hour, hopefully without repeating myself. I talked about everything under the sun, and as I talked, more of what is under the sun was revealed to me. Toward the end, talking in this way—and seeing by their faces and responses that I was getting through—seemed entirely miraculous. *As miraculous as writing.*

I will give you an example: I did not think I could survive the last talk. Talk number nine. We'd flown into town at one o'clock, *sans* breakfast or lunch; the talk was at two. On the way into the building I'd seen lines of people patiently filing into the auditorium. I sat in a huge vacant room someone had led me to, regretting the intensely spicy food I had been eating for two weeks, which made me feel bloated and dim, and attempted to gather my thoughts; thanking all the Buddhas who ever lived for insisting on meditation. I had ten minutes.

Even as I approached the lectern I had no idea what I would say. I was committed, however, to opening my mouth. After that . . . it was up to a power greater than mine. I looked out into a sea of alert, curious, interested, and I think on some level surprised faces. Who was this little brown woman, her graying hair tinted the color of autumn straw, with nothing in her hands? And as I looked at them, all Koreans, all appearing healthy and well-off, and now living in a new city built after the old one had been bombed into bits, memory of one of my brothers came into my mind. I recalled a photograph he'd sent to us during the Korean War. He was falling out of a plane.

He was falling out of the plane because he'd joined the Air Force after being expelled from high school in the eleventh grade because he had slapped the principal. I suppose he'd been taught, by the U.S. military, how to parachute "behind enemy lines." That must have been what he was training for, in the photograph. But how had these people in front of me, whom he'd never heard of until a month or so before he parachuted down among them, become his enemy? And that is what I found myself talking about. About my brother's obvious anger and *hurt* as a teenager, about his youth. *He was so young.* About his lasting dislike of Asians. And how that dislike, which had so startled me when I took him on a stroll through Japan Town in San Francisco, was undoubtedly the result of his *fear*, to be so distant from his rural home in Georgia, little more than a child, among people who were better off—except for the destructiveness of war—and with a longer history, than any, including white Americans, that he had ever seen. *And that they would have been trying to kill him.* The ancient universities and temples still standing after years of bombing would have astonished him. It must have puzzled him endlessly that he was asked to kill people who were of color and that these people of color owned their country. He must have admired, even as he dreaded it, their ability to fight. I wonder if he ever understood, beyond the propaganda, what the Koreans, Northern Communist and Southern anti-Communist, were fighting about. Or who benefited, ultimately, from the war that lasted so long and caused so much harm. I wondered if he had killed some of the relatives of the people in the audience. Had he done terrible things to children or to women? When he returned, there was little he could tell us. And now I marveled at how difficult coming home must have been for him. Talking to his family about Korea would have been more challenging than telling us about the moon. We could see the moon.

During the question-and-answer session the topic of a quota of young Koreans being sent to fight in Iraq came up. As a colony of the U.S., though a seemingly prosperous one, this is a requirement. Wars that the U.S. fights are considered South Korea's.

Don't send your children anywhere, I said.

It was only after I returned home and discussed this new awareness of my brother's life with an older sibling that I learned even more of what was "under the sun." Her husband, she said, fought in Korea. His best friend was blown up right next to him. He couldn't talk about it, so he drank. He was also very violent, though I did not mention this. And our older brother, she continued sadly, who so rarely says anything, was also a soldier there.

This is what I mean about this time we are living in. Although only 7 percent of Americans have passports—a shocking realization since we seem to be everywhere—99 percent of us have television or the Internet. There are still libraries, bookstores and books. *Documentaries. There are still teachers.* To begin our long journey toward balance as a planet, we have only to study the world and its peoples, to see they are *so like ourselves! To trust that this is so.* That different clothes and religions do not create people who can escape from humanity. When we face the peoples of the world with open hands, and in honesty and fearlessness speak what is in our memories and our hearts, the dots connect themselves.

You may say to me: But Alice, all these connecting dots connect disasters. True enough, but they also connect millions of people who worked hard and beautifully to prevent, defeat, or transform them.

The best of times.

Being in Korea, which I'd only "seen" on *M*A*S*H*, a television program that often made me laugh, I remembered my first trip abroad as a nineteen-year-old. I went to Russia, part of the then–Soviet Union. I had no idea what to expect; were white people the same the world over? I wondered. Would these white people in Russia think it "natural" to segregate me from themselves, as white Southerners did in the United States? Imagine my surprise when they did not, but instead embraced me the same as they embraced everybody else, with a kiss on each cheek and a bouquet of flowers. I knew in that moment that war with them, which we were constantly on the verge of, had to be the least intelligent move on Earth.

I felt the same a couple of years later in Africa. The people in Kenya and Uganda (pre–Idi Amin and Daniel Arap-Moi) were the friendliest, most gentle people I'd ever met. They cooked delicious food, too, and created lovely music. The thought of anyone harming them because their leaders might force them into war was painful. In fact, while I was in East Africa the only things I saw that needed "attacking" were poverty and ignorance, especially when it came to women: it was there that I first learned of the genital cutting of young women and even babies in an attempt to dominate them and control their sexuality. I would later write about this practice, an assault on the health of the entire people, as I discovered, in my novel *Possessing the Secret of Joy.*

It is criminal, and immoral, I believe, to send our children—and nineteen- and twenty-year-olds are still our children—to fight and kill people they've never seen, never met, often never heard of. Like my brother, many of the young who are sent to maim and murder others like themselves may never even have glanced, on a map, at the places they are going. How like my brother these young Koreans seemed. Korea is just as far from Iraq—in culture if not distance—as it is from Georgia, U.S.A. Why should young Koreans die for an American empire that attacked Iraq in the first place not because Iraq had attacked the U.S.A. but because the U.S. intends to possess and control Iraq's oil?

An enlightened rage is building in the peoples of the world and it is antiwar. Never before have we seen war so clearly: its horror and stupidity and waste. We watch, those of us in the West, mostly on television, unimaginable blunders of planning and strategy; we walk past our rapidly deteriorating hospitals and schools while reading about the ten billion dollars a day, or is it a month, or is it a minute, spent on war in what is obviously the wrong country, in newspapers that report this news, it seems to us, casually. We feel helpless in that moment, but we do not feel ignorant. That is a great gain.

It is bad enough, we feel, that our young, often poor, badly educated and frequently desperate young men are forced into war; they have few alternatives. But to see our young women, likewise disadvantaged, leaving their babies behind in order to fight—and sometimes facing harassment, assault and rape from their own male compatriots, in addition to the dangers and malevolence of war, feels like more than we can bear.

What does it mean to love one's child and not be able to protect him or her? Cindy Sheehan, who lost her son Casey in the war in Iraq, demonstrates the power of grief. Holding vigils outside the president's ranch and elsewhere, demanding that he sit with her; speaking everywhere, telling the truth of her sadness and exhibiting her fury, she lends us courage by her persistence. We have slumbered a long time believing the lies of those in power. Sending our children to fight those who might have been their playmates. And we know that those in power must spend a lot of their time laughing at us. Take a moment to think about how gullible, how innocent, we must seem to them. Moved about the world to do their bidding, like pieces on a chessboard. But in this time we are beginning to see and hear from mothers and fathers who assume the role of Those Who Also Know. The world is getting its Elders back.

Sit for a moment and consider what it means to be aware; let yourself feel the many ways you have been morally and politically manipulated and tricked. Consider your own part in this. Return to a place in recent memory, perhaps to September 11, 2001. How do you feel about the way events unfolded? What would you do differently if such an event happened again? What have you learned about "leaders" and "facts" and your own willingness to believe, or disbelieve, what others tell you in a time of fear and, especially, of mourning?

The world is as beautiful as it ever was. It is changing, but then it always has been. This is a good time to change, and remain beautiful, with it.

1.

Three Fates

Graduation Address
Agnes Scott College
2000

Some years ago, on December 17, 1996, at 7:16 in the morning, I witnessed my first birth. To see a baby being born was something I had wanted since I was a child and heard the mysterious information that babies came out of women's bodies. *Who could believe this?*

I had been invited to this birth by the midwife, a friend of mine, and by the mother and grandmother of the baby involved.

I arrived at the birth mother's home in the early dawn—the exact time, it seems to me, that one should be summoned. Four o'clock in the morning, if I recall correctly. As I mounted the steps leading to the mother's door, I heard her cries.

This seemed as it should be. I felt—the world

being as populated with humans as it is—that I should have been hearing these cries before. It is astonishing that at every moment a new person, many new persons, are being born. And that we do not hear this, so well hidden has the act of birth become.

The living room I entered, after removing my shoes, seemed ancient, even cavelike, as friends of the young mother sat about in clusters, quietly talking, or making tea and coffee for those just entering.

I was asked by my midwife friend to hold the light, and, as labor progressed, I was privileged to see each of its stages. The young mother was oblivious to all but her pain; those of us helping her were so attuned to her feelings that, during contractions, we instinctively panted and breathed with her. Until the last moment I could not believe that a baby would be the result of what I was seeing.

Four hours after my arrival, the baby dropped out of his mother into the soft palms of my midwife friend; in one fluid motion she laid him on his mother's breast. It was a beautiful birth. The mother, only sixteen years old, had demonstrated an authority and courage that were pure warriorship.

As the birth of the baby was announced outside the bedroom in which it occurred, the men of the tribe—the baby was born into an extended Native

American family—quietly began to make breakfast, which they served to the women who had participated in the birthing, and later to the clan of people who gathered to celebrate the birth throughout the day. I left this experience feeling blessed, inspired, somehow purified.

The next baby I encountered was in central Mexico, where I have a home and where I sometimes go to write. As a near, quickly reached, Third World country, Mexico is ideal for me because it offers a constant reminder of all that is transpiring in over two-thirds of the so-called developing world. This little girl was six months old when we met. I fell for her instantly. Perhaps it was the elegant baldness of her head. Her direct, curious gaze. Her scent of happiness. Not since my own daughter was born many years before had I felt such joy as I beheld a new addition to our world.

Her parents are quite well-off, and so she has a nurse and a nursery, her own pristine wing, located in her parents' spectacular sea-cliff house. She has excellent food, beautiful, tiny dresses and piles of toys. She will be raised to be upper-class. This of course worries me.

It worries me partly because of the third baby I encountered during this same period. This was the six-week-old daughter of the woman who occasionally keeps house for me; a struggling middle-aged mother of three who'd recently married a man who convinced her to try to give him a son.

On my way to visit her and to bring gifts for baby and mother, I pondered the baby's future. The house into which she was born was as different from the previous house as could be imagined: essentially one room, with what appeared to be a dirt floor, in part of a crumbling building that rises very close to a dusty and noisy road.

The furniture in the house consisted of one bed, a table and a couple of chairs, all old and much used. When the mother went to get the baby for me to see, it was as though she rummaged among a pile of rags on the bed before lifting her up, which she did with pride. After talking with her for a while it became clear that her marriage was troubled and that her body was not healing properly from the birth. I urged her to return to the hospital, noting not only her lack of energy, but that the child seemed languid and weak as well.

The first child's mother is too young and unskilled to take on the task of raising a child. Fortunately, the child's grandmother is present, as is the native community into which he was born. This child will have many challenges, as a Native American, in a world in which much of what might have gone into strengthening him has deliberately been destroyed by the dominant culture. His primary obstacle in life might well be despair. On the other hand, he enters a community that is becoming ever more conscious of what it is, what its struggle to survive is, and also what its commitment to its own values must be. It is also a community that, in its essence, venerates beauty, justice and love.

The second baby's parents, it seemed to me—with their baby's spotless white nursery in a very casual and colorful Mexico—are attempting to seal her off from the raw poverty that exists ten minutes away. I dread the day when she awakens to her overwhelming privilege in a country whose children, materially speaking, often have little. I dread even more, however, the possibility that by the time she is an adult, the material disparity between herself and others will have no meaning for her. That she will walk over and around and through her nurse, the servants, and the population of poor Mexicans—as many rich Mexicans do—without seeing their condition of poverty, or even really seeing them. This would be a disaster in one born so beautiful and so inspiring of love.

If I were writing a fairy tale, I would say that the little girl born across the way, on the bed that resembled a pile of rags, might grow up to be the servant of the rich little girl in the sea-cliff castle who is nonetheless at this stage very sweet. The little rich girl, let us call her Hope, would resist becoming the spoiled snob I fear she might become, and instead she and the poor girl, let us call her Joy, would become friends so loyal to each other that Hope's parents would not know what to make of it. Hope would quietly teach Joy everything there is to know about place settings and table manners;

horseback riding and society dances. Joy would teach Hope all there is to know about card-playing, algebra, swimming in the river, and how to shop in the pueblo without encountering one word of disrespect. They would be mutually disgusted that Joy's parents were so poor and Hope's parents so outlandishly rich. They would plot, from an early age, to discover a way to equalize things.

Along would come, perhaps, the third child, now a fully grown Native American man, a warrior like his mother. He would join the two women. Together they would open a school to teach the children of the very poor, many of them indigenous. They would agitate for economic democracy in Mexico. They would be vilified in the press as Communists and chased out of town. They would take to the mountains. From there, they, along with the thousands coming to join them, would begin the second Mexican revolution. Perhaps they would model their rebellion on the Zapatista movement, ongoing, presently, in the Mexican state of Chiapas.

What will in fact be the lives of these children? This is the cry that must wake us from sleep.

Since you invited me to Agnes Scott College on this special day—the day in which you launch yourselves into new and ever more challenging studies of and endeavors in the world—I will feel free in giving you the advantage of my own harsh opinion about having children just now. *I believe there should be a moratorium on the birth of children.* That not one more child should be born on this planet until certain conditions are met. Perhaps the most important of these is that the several missing pounds of plutonium—the most deadly substance ever concocted by man; the inhalation of a single particle causes cancer—must be found. I believe it was the valiant Dr. Helen Caldicott who alerted us to the fact that it is missing, just as she has worked for over a decade to warn us of the lethal effects of nuclear power and nuclear waste. Where is this awful substance? Who has stolen it? For what purpose will they use it? And what about the information we now have about the use of plutonium in fueling rockets, which, as we know, sometimes self-destruct, scattering their fuel and the bodies of the crew over the face of Mother Earth?

In fact, in a recent article it was announced that NASA will launch something called the Cassini probe. It will carry 72.3 pounds of plutonium-238. Enough to disable and kill millions of people on earth, *if anything goes wrong.* Apparently the scientists at NASA wish to visit Saturn. *Do you?* A visit that could cost us our lives. A visit Saturn itself has not initiated. The colonizing mind invites itself wherever it wishes to intrude; it is a worthwhile practice for the coming millennium to train ourselves away from such a mind.

Begin, then, with tracking the use and whereabouts of the missing and badly misused plutonium. If we do not find the plutonium that is missing and contain that which is being misused, there is not much hope that any of our children will live free from pain into a healthy old age. Millions of them will not live at all.

From there, work to make the routine drinking of bottled water a distant nightmare. Water was not meant to be polluted, any more than human blood, which is mostly water, is meant to be contaminated. How dare we bring anyone into the world who must, anywhere on earth, run from rain? Native people have always maintained that water—like trees, rocks, and the earth itself—has emotions. *Think how it must feel.* We must learn respect for water and teach this respect to the billions of humans already here.

And then, there are the lives of the other animals—humans being only one animal, and a minority—to consider. These must be honored, freed from their cages, their lands returned to them, with our deepest apologies and most heartfelt reparations. I recently read about an experiment in which chimpanzees were taught enough sign language to speak with humans. One of the things they divulged was that they liked a movie called *Field of Dreams.* I have not seen this movie: what moved me was their enjoyment and understanding of it. I want children who are already born to understand that there is much to distrust about the zoo.

There is much work to be done, sister and brother Earthlings. But we have, if we work earnestly enough, all of eternity to do it. I personally take comfort in this thought. In fact, it is by working on these issues that an eternity might be ours. And I leave it to you to consider this, for a time in your life when you will sit on a green hill somewhere and consciously dream up a future for your very own child.

You will have children, the majority of you. Some of you may already have them. You will not listen to me at all. I myself do not listen to me. And this makes me laugh. It is such a classic predicament of human nature. Even as I enumerate the perils we face as a planet, the instability of every single system, the irresponsibility of an obsolete "leadership," the lethal nature of "progress," I find myself longing—hence my recent fixation on babies—to be a grandmother.

I say to my daughter more frequently than she appreciates: Where is my grandchild?

I am not wrong in this. I know how wonderful babies are. How much learning and growth and humor they bring. Babies come empty-handed, but bringing so many gifts! That is why so many of us want them. My own baby's birth was a miracle from which I shall never recover. The way she felt and smelled—where in fact do babies come from?—will be forever a part of why I adore life. *Life is audacious.*

What then does such a mixed message mean?

It means consciousness about all that is happening around you, that endangers Life. The One Big Life all of us share. Essentially it means hard work. Our Earth home will be insecure and uncertain for many millennia. Despite our anxieties, we will have to learn to find comfort and solace here. Not by cordoning ourselves off from others, not by killing others or stealing their resources, but by learning to sit in council with them as we discuss what has become our common destiny on a planet nearly wrecked by the behavior of human beings. In this regard, it is helpful to witness the growing formation of councils the world over: of women, of elders, of grandmothers, of wise people who love the earth and look forward with apprehension and caring to the coming generations.

So, young women of Agnes Scott College, I salute your great accomplishment, that you have studied long hours in preparation for your graduation day. That you love the world so much you have taken the time and made the effort to prepare yourselves to serve it. Have your work in the world, and have your children. Only one, please, out of respect for the weight we are to our Mother. But be aware that the other children of the world are your responsibility as well. You must learn to see them, to feel them, as yours. Until you do, there is no way you can make your own child feel safe. And because when you do, you will join the rest of the world in cleaning up the rivers, clearing the air, saving the trees, and finding and containing every ounce of the missing and misappropriated plutonium.

What happens to the three children in my non–fairy tale will be largely up to adults of the world, people like you.

I have named the rich little girl Hope. The poor little girl Joy. I will now name the Native American little boy (who became my godchild) Song. Here is a poem for them:

The Day You Are Born

On the day that you are born
Beautiful beings
Those who love you
Tremble
We tremble because
We are afraid

You are so mysterious
Beautiful beings
And we do not know
Who sent you
Nor do we know
Where you are from

Imagine how perplexed
You make us
As your bald (or hairy) head
Slides gradually
Into view
Between your mother's
Thighs
And we hold our breaths
As, after so much pain to her, you casually
Drop.

What struggles you have already
Endured
Just
To get here!
How could we not
Welcome you
In awe?

Watching you emerge
Into the light
We wonder if what we see
Is even possible.
If we were religious
In the way inherited from our parents
We would cross
Ourselves.
And remembering that the cross
Symbolizes that place
Where spirit and matter

Meet
We might cross ourselves
Anyway
Out of respect
For the crossroad
Your birth
Presents
For your mother
And you.

Oh, little ones
Who will one day
Be
So much taller than us
Let us pledge
On your sweet heads
To make a better show
Of things
Than we have done.

Let us promise
To take courage
From the mysterious
Nature of your
Journey.
Let us acknowledge
In all humility
That regardless of
Your status in life
It is we
Who are blessed.

We do not know the beginning
Or the end
We only see the middle of things
Which is our own life.

Perhaps you are a part of
The force
That is coming to help
Us
Rearrange our world
To make it better
We pray that this is
So.

That you have come back
To help heal the confusion
You left behind
So many lifetimes
Ago.

And that you come
Bringing all
We need
To get the job
Done:

Joy, Hope, Song.

We must abandon the notion that we become grandparents only when our own children give birth. In the same way that all adults are ultimately responsible for all of earth's children, grandparents come into being when we realize we are responsible for all the grandchildren on the earth. This does not mean we can single-handedly feed, house and clothe the eleven or so million orphans in Africa, for instance, whose parents have died of AIDS, but it does mean we find ways to connect and relate to as many endangered children on the globe as possible. There are many organizations already formed to make this connection possible. I am particularly drawn to those that teach self-reliance and sustainability. One of my favorites is Heifer International. Each year, through this organization, I am able to send cows, sheep, water buffalo, chickens, pigs, ducks and rabbits to families with children around the globe. As someone who grew up on a farm I know exactly what I'm sending.

What I would like this and other organizations to consider is the institution, at the many orphanages in Africa and around the world, of small farms stocked with animals for the children to own and care for. Nothing will ever replace their parents, but having animals to tend will ameliorate the loneliness.

I am also an honorary co-founder of Women for Women International, which supports women and their children who have been victims of war. If you are past fifty, take some time to contemplate becoming a grandparent. To what children in what part of the world are you particularly drawn? How are these children faring? What would you do to help them if you lived nearby? Can you find a way to do at least some of that from far away?

If you are fortunate enough to have grandchildren of your own, that is to say by blood, introduce them to these other children that you perhaps passionately love. Encourage them to join you in attempting to care for them. Only when these other children are safe in the world will your grandchildren be safe. Explain to your grandchildren how this works.

From the time I was a teenager I have done my best to protect Cuban children, African children, and children of the poor, of whatever color. When I am with them my "grandmother gene" comes vibrantly alive within me. It is a longing for the healthy self and world that humanity is capable of providing for everyone, and in that moment, because I feel its possibility so intensely, I can envision a different, more glowingly perfect future for the planet. I wish this experience, which is actually a kind of ecstasy, for you as well.

2.

Childhood

One evening my daughter came to pick me up from the country; I had been expecting her for several hours. Almost as soon as she came through the door I asked if she knew how potatoes look before they are dug out of the ground. She wasn't sure. Then I will show you in the morning before we head back to the city, I told her.

I had begun to harvest my potato crop the day before. In the spring I planted five varieties: my favorite, yellow Finn, but also Yukon gold, Peruvian purple, Irish white, and red new. Even though the summer had been chilly and there was morning shade from the large oak at the front of the garden, the potatoes came up quickly and developed into healthy plants. José, who helps me in the garden, had shoveled an extra collar of humus around each plant and I was delighted as each of them began to bloom. It had been years since I planted potatoes. I planted them in the garden I'd previously devoted to corn because I have a schedule that often means I am far away from my garden at just the time my corn becomes ripe. Having sped home to my garden three years in a row to a plot of over-matured, tasteless corn, I decided to plant potatoes instead, thinking the worst that could happen, if I were delayed elsewhere, would be a handful of potatoes nibbled by gophers or moles.

I had been dreading going back to the city, where I had more things to do than I cared to think about; I sat in the swing on the deck thinking hard about what would be my last supper in the country. I had bought some green peas from the roadside stand a few miles from my house, there were chard and kale flourishing a few steps from my door, and I had brought up corn from a small hopeful planting in a lower garden. Tasting the corn, however, I discovered it had, as I'd feared, lost its sweetness and turned into starch. Then I remembered my potatoes! I grabbed a shovel, went out to the garden, and began to dig. The experience I had had digging the potatoes, before turning them into half of a delicious meal, was one I wanted my daughter to know.

After boiling them, I ate my newly dug potatoes, several small yellow Finns and two larger Peruvian purples, with only a dressing of butter. Organic butter with a dash of sea salt, that reminded me of the butter my mother and grandmother used to make. As I ate the mouthwatering meal I remembered them sitting patiently beside the brown or creamy white churn, moving the dasher up and down in a steady rhythmic motion, until flecks of butter appeared at the top of the milk. These flecks grew until eventually there was enough butter to make a small mound. We owned a beautiful handcrafted butter press. It was sometimes my job to press its wooden carving of flowers into the hardening butter, making a cheerful and elegant design.

In the morning, just before packing the car for the ride to the city, I harvested an abundance of Chardonnay grapes, greenish-silver and refreshingly sweet; a bucket of glistening eggplant; an armful of collards and chard and kale; some dark green and snake-like cucumbers, plus a small sack of figs and half a dozen late-summer peaches. Then I took my daughter out to the neat rows of potatoes, all beginning to turn brown. Using the shovel to scrape aside the dirt, I began to reveal, very slowly and carefully, the golden and purple potatoes that rested just beneath the plants. She was enchanted. It's just like . . . it's just like . . . she said. It's just like finding gold, I offered, with glee. Yes! she said, her eyes wide.

Though my daughter is now in her thirties, her enthusiasm reminded me of my own when I was probably no more than three. My parents, exemplary farmers and producers of fine vegetables in garden and field, had enchanted me early in just this same way. As I scraped dirt aside from another potato plant and watched as my daughter began to fill her skirt with our treasure, I was taken back to a time when I was very young, perhaps too young even to speak. The very first memory I have is certainly pre-verbal; I was lifted up by my father or an older brother, very large and dark and shining men, and encouraged to pick red plums from a heavily bearing tree. The next is of going with my parents, in a farm wagon, to a watermelon patch that in memory seems to have been planted underneath pine trees. A farmer myself now, I realize this couldn't have been true. It is likely that to get to the watermelon patch we had to go through the pines. In any case, and perhaps this was pre-verbal as well, I remember the absolute wonder of rolling along in a creaky wooden wagon that was pulled by obedient if indifferent mules, arriving at a vast field and being taken down and placed out of the way as my brothers and parents began to find watermelon after watermelon and to bring them back, apparently, as gifts for me! In a short time the wagon was filled with large green watermelons. And there were still dozens more left to grow larger in the field! How had this happened? What miracle was this?

As soon as they finished filling the wagon, my father broke open a gigantic melon right on the spot. The "spot" being a handy boulder as broad as a table that happened to reside there, underneath the shady pines, beside the field. We were all given pieces of its delicious red and thirst-quenching heart. He then carefully, from my piece, removed all the glossy black seeds.

If you eat one of these, he joked, poking at my protruding tummy, a watermelon just like this will grow inside you.

It will? My eyes were probably enormous. I must have looked shocked.

Everyone laughed.

If you put the seed into the ground, it will grow, said an older brother, who could never bear to see me deceived. That's how all of these watermelons came to be here. We planted them.

It seemed too wonderful for words. *Too incredible to be believed.* One thing seemed as astonishing as another. That a watermelon could grow inside me, if I ate a seed, and that watermelons grew from seeds put in the ground!

When I think of my childhood at its best it is of this magic that I think. Of having a family that daily worked with nature to produce the extraordinary, and yet they were all so casual about it, and never failed to find my wonderment amusing. Years later I would write poems and essays about the way growing up in the country seemed the best of all possible worlds, regardless of the hardships that made getting by year to year, especially for a family of color in the South half a century ago, a heroic affair.

I have experienced many difficulties and hardships in my life and yet despair is a state in which I rarely remain for long. This is largely because despair cannot share the same space as wonder, and it is wonder that I have had from childhood, and in abundance. From the moment I saw that a plum grew out of a brown-colored, dry-looking branch, and a watermelon came from a green stem attached to a plant that was rooted in the dark earth, "heaven" as described by the pastor of our church (somewhere beyond earth) became irrelevant. I was already in the only heaven that mattered to me, and I knew it.

This sense of the magic of Nature has encouraged all of my environmental understanding and activism. It is the reason I believe all our children, whether two years old or forty, should be encouraged to look, really look, at what they are seeing every day: incredible improbabilities, miracles— plums, watermelons, tulips, turnips—that are, on our planet, that radiant blue orb, exceedingly ordinary, though obviously divine.

In fact, a useful meditation would be to sit with your child or grandchild and eat a peach together.

The peach is perhaps my favorite fruit, though I love them all. First have the child hold and smell the peach, remembering that it is in full sun that its scent is strongest. This might be a good time to teach how important it is not to refrigerate fruit, unless it is essential to storing it. That it is best just off the tree, fully ripened, or ripened in an airy fruit bowl until its scent begins to permeate the air. Let your child or grandchild (or your neighbor's child or grandchild) sniff and feel the fuzz of the peach. When he or she bites into the peach let the juice run down her or his chin. Ask a simple question: Is that good? Another simple question: Where do you suppose this comes from? The child will not know of course, any more than you do.

What is left then is simply to enjoy.

You might ask: Do we want this experience of goodness to last forever and for everyone on earth to have it? It is very likely the child will say yes. This is your opportunity to gently share ideas about how this might be accomplished.

3.

When Life Descends
into the Pit

At the end of *By the Light of My Father's Smile*, Susannah, a writer and by now a very old woman, has died at home in bed, surrounded by her friends. One by one they come forward to say good-bye to her body, and to cover her with boughs of trees, dry grass and twigs.

Her sister, Magdalena, who has died decades earlier, but who has been compelled, as an angel or ghost, to be with her sister at her death in order to correct a terrible wrong she did her as a child, watches in horror as Susannah and all her books, records and tapes are methodically set on fire. Magdalena cannot believe her sister intends to erase her life.

Susannah, however, also an angel or ghost, has learned an important pagan lesson about how destructive is the need to be remembered, and is gleeful to watch her own body burn.

As she watches, Magdalena says: The flames from her burning house were bright, and reminded me of a poem:

When life descends into the pit
I must become my own candle
Willingly burning myself
To light up the darkness
Around me.

By the Light of My Father's Smile acknowledges that there are many pits into which life has fallen at this point. Almost too many to name or even to think about. There is the pit of loneliness, so widespread in this postmodern world; the pit of violence, in which our children are slowly drowning; the pit of fear, as we realize how trapped we are in our cities, our towns and our streets, and even in the countryside, where men seem now to be almost always armed, and women know in our bones that we are never safe.

By the Light of My Father's Smile looks into the pit into which sexuality has fallen. It is calling fathers in particular to come and witness the catastrophe into which this most basic expression of self-love and love-of-other has fallen. It maintains that female children are dying from the abandonment they suffer from their fathers the moment they become recognizable as sexual beings; sometimes this recognition comes at or even before birth. It says our unacknowledged longing for our father's blessing of what we desire quite frequently drives us mad.

I cannot speak of this novel and its affirmation of sexuality without returning at least briefly to the novel I wrote preceding it, *Possessing the Secret of Joy*. It was in that novel that I experienced the full awareness of the fall of our human sexual integrity, especially as women. I must speak of the grief and pain I felt as I researched and then wrote that novel about the genital mutilation—systematically, methodically, unfeelingly—of millions of small girls and adult women, personified in the character Tashi, a tribal African woman who elects to be mutilated because she has been brainwashed by her culture to believe this act alone validates her existence as a female.

If this could happen to a hundred million women and girls alive today, across the globe, without protest, without comment, without any but the most isolated outrage, what did it mean to be a woman anywhere in the world, at this particular time on earth?

And so this novel, *By the Light of My Father's Smile*, began there, in outrage, in grief, and in the understanding that our human sexual life—because of genital cutting (and sewing), because of rape, because of AIDS and the chilling fear of disease, because of gender abuse of all kinds, because of the thorough domination of women and girls over much of the earth—has fallen into the pit.

And, to be completely adult, there may be nothing any of us can do about it.

Being a novelist, however, I opted to try.

When my child was small, I sent her to an alternative school called New Traditions that was near our house in San Francisco. In this school there was an emphasis on sharing, on noncompetitive behavior, on gender equality. It had seemed to me for a long time that the old traditions of domination and control are leading us to our death. And in fact it was a joy to see the children at this school blossom into adults who appear to have little interest in "getting ahead" or relating to something so stressful as a "fast track."

The Mundo, a tribe of mixed-race black and Indian people I have created in this novel, are likewise unimpressed by a world concerned primarily with exploitation and monetary gain. They treasure instead their relatedness to the Earth, and their own rituals, ceremonies and ways. That there are people in the world who mutilate their children genitally is horrible, unbelievable, to them. They are people who kiss where others cut; behavior that has marked them for extinction.

And so they teach the father in this book, a man who has become an unwilling prisoner of a puritanical Christianity, and who believes his daughter's sexuality is evil, that sexuality is instead a mystery, a blessing and a wise teacher of the Self. In the end, they lead him back to his children, his daughters, whose sexual wounds, whose soul wounds, he is deeply responsible for.

Ultimately *By the Light of My Father's Smile* affirms the thought that though life as we know it has indeed fallen into the pit, each of us has knowledge of how to live life differently that no one taught us, and that we can find this knowledge inside ourselves and put it to use. That there is Mundo consciousness—the desire to honor instead of degrade, to kiss instead of cut—in every one of us.

This is a time when teachings of all traditions are available to us. If we are lucky, we will have close friends of other cultures who will tell us, in phone call, letter, or e-mail, of a wise understanding of life passed on by earlier generations. The Beloved Woman of the Cherokee people, former Principal Chief of the Cherokee Nation, Wilma Mankiller, with whom I became friends many years ago, sent the following message from the Onondaga: "Take care how you place your moccasins upon the Earth, step with care, for the faces of the future generations are looking up from the Earth waiting their turn for life."

Sit with this message. Whose hopeful faces are you standing on?

There is another saying from a Native American people that moves me: "Relative, shift your teepee, Mother Earth needs sunlight." When I first heard this, I cried with joy. Nowhere else had I heard expressed my sense of Earth's suffering at having so much of itself covered with heavy buildings. Teepees of course are not heavy, they're quite light. That a compassionate ancestor still thought this too much weight for the Mother to bear, without being shifted occasionally, stirred my heart with love.

Consider the Ice Age. The people in the North desperate for shelter; their use of caves, some of which they decorated beautifully with pictures of life before the great ice came. Contemplate their joy when the ice receded, though it was still very cold. Think how natural it must have been, and ingenious too, to build housing that resembled caves. Something substantial, often of stone, built to keep them warm.

Now there are heavy houses everywhere and more of them being built. In fact, it is only when more houses are being constructed that some countries consider their economies healthy. Yet each house is a heavy footprint on the Earth. Just as all our possessions represent—if we cannot learn ways of sharing them—a weight and a clutter that often means the faces of future generations will look up into darkness and the pressure on the Earth of "things." My family had no home of our own when I was a child—we were tenant farmers and quite poor—and therefore I inherited an intense house hunger, which I have fed by owning several. Only one of them did I build myself, and I will never build another, even though that one was built off the ground, and sunlight can indeed reach some areas underneath it.

It seems wiser to do as hermit crabs do, find a shell and inhabit it. This is more ecological too. To use what is still beautiful and sound, repair what is broken; in a word, renovate housing that already exists. And as houses and buildings fall, clear the debris, make firewood or build other useful things with it, but leave the land free and breathing. I realize there will be new buildings placed on the site of the World Trade Center, whose towers were destroyed on September 11th, 2001, but I consider it a backward step. A monstrously heavy step on the faces coming forward.

One of my favorite indulgences when I visit any large and heavy American city is to imagine what the place was like two and three hundred years ago. The huge old trees, the clean and shining rivers, the fish so thick an explorer exclaimed one could walk across a river on their backs. And the human faces that assumed they would always find a clearing in the grass.

As you sit, make peace also with the reality that, after you die, it won't matter to you how you are remembered; you will not be here to experience it.

All the grand things that you do or say, all the sky-scrapers you build and cover with gold, your elegant tombstone, all will be completely forgotten eventually. Even your children, and their children too, will be forgotten. That being so, perhaps it is best to begin to erase your presence well before you leave the scene. This can help make a space for one of those faces coming up through the grass.

Contemplate giving away possessions and practice giving away your self. Talk to the young; offer whatever you have learned that might be of use. Sponsor students and artists of whatever age, whenever possible. Artists and seekers of knowledge often face enormous challenges just to keep themselves and their visions alive; this is especially true if they are poor. When you give of yourself to them you make a wide clearing in a world that is too often overgrown with bad art and substandard education. Keep track of family members; talk with them, work and plan for the future with them, vacation with them, take them with you when you have something joyful to share.

In deep meditation the self, the ego busy with its many projects, completely disappears. It is the most delightful experience imaginable. Perhaps death will be like this. You are sitting there, but light is streaming right through the place where you sit. This experience can be had in motion, too, and is the experience we have when giving ourselves away. It is as if we are dissolving into everything and everyone around us and we recognize the illusion of separateness. And when someone thanks you for something, you thank *them*, because you realize it is only their acceptance of your gift that allows you to give.

Sit with the thought of erasing yourself so that others might more gracefully arrive. One easy way to do this is to imagine the spot you are sitting in without you. It will remain full of itself, which contains also, somehow, the invisible essence of you.

4.

All Praises to the Pause; The Universal Moment of Reflection

Commencement Address
California Institute of Integral Studies
San Francisco, California
May 19, 2002

After Completion:

> *He brakes his wheels.*
> *He gets his tail in the water.*
> *No blame.*

One of the many gifts I received from strangers after writing *The Color Purple* twenty years ago was a bright yellow volume of the *I Ching*. It opened to the sixty-third hexagram: *After Completion*. This is a time when a major transition from confusion to order has been completed—for instance, it would apply to this moment when you have concluded your studies at CIIS—and everything is (at last!) in its proper place (you are gradu-ating) even in particulars. Interestingly, according to the *I Ching*, this is a time not of relaxation, but of caution:

> In times following a great transition, everything is pressing forward, striving in the direction of de-velopment and progress. But this pressing for-ward at the beginning is not good; it overshoots the mark and leads with certainty to loss and col-lapse. Therefore a man (or woman) of strong character does not allow himself (herself) to be infected by the general intoxication but checks his (her) course in time. He (She, They) may in-deed not remain altogether untouched by the dis-astrous consequences of the general pressure, but . . . is hit only from behind like a fox that, having crossed the water, at the last minute gets its tail wet. He (She) will not suffer any real harm, be-cause his (her) behavior has been correct.

The *I Ching* is a compass of great value. Un-canny in its ability to share its Wisdom at just the moment it is required. How many friends, even best and closest friends, can do that?

What it is referring to in this hexagram is some-thing that I am going to call "the pause." The mo-ment when something major is accomplished and we are so relieved to finally be done with it that we are already rushing, at least mentally, into The Future. Wisdom, however, requests a pause. If we cannot give ourselves such a pause, the Universe will likely give it to us. In the form of illness, in the form of a massive mercury in retrograde, in the form of our car breaking down, our roof starting to leak, our garden starting to dry up. Our government collapsing. And we find ourselves required to stop, to sit down, to reflect. This is the time of "the pause," the universal place of stopping. The universal moment of reflection.

I am here today to encourage you not to fear it. And why is it important to be told, to be reminded not to fear the pause? Because some of the most courageous people on earth are scared of it, as I have been myself. Why is this? It is because the pause has nothing in it; it feels empty. It feels like we have been jettisoned into wide open, empty space. We can not see an end to it. Not seeing an end to it, or for that matter, not even understanding a beginning or a need for it, we panic. We may decide to make war, for instance, in the moment the Universe has given us to reflect. By the time we recover from our hasty activity a thousand small children may be lying dead at our feet.

Sometimes there is a feeling of not being able to continue. That, in this pause, whichever one it is, there is no movement. No encouragement to move, at all.

There is a poem someone sent me that speaks beautifully of this. It is called "A Blessing" and is by Stephen Philbrick. It was sent to me as a gift for having done a benefit reading for the Women's Fund of Western Massachusetts. I was experiencing a pause of major proportions when I did the benefit, with no idea this poem would be the treasure I would receive. I dedicate it with much *metta*, (a Buddhist term that might translate as caring, or loving-kindness) to you.

A Blessing

Don't try so hard.
It comes in a shiver sometimes,
Sometimes in a winter windowpane,
Wild with the unseeable
Frozen there in ice:
The shapes above clouds,
The score and the libretto of wind,
The plot of waves.
Don't try so hard.
Sometimes it falls,
A flake at a time,
Into your life while you're asleep.
Sometimes it comes as a winter
Blankness,
Waiting for storm, or ice, or thaw,
Or even wind,
And then the still air groans,
And the trees crack,

The swamp shudders,
And the woods thrill.
Sometimes it comes when you least
Expect it.
And sometimes it doesn't.
Quiet, still, no voice (even small),
No whirlwind, no reply; no burning.
Just a bare winter bush.
This is God, too.

The space between stars,
Where noise goes to die,
And the space between atoms,
Where the charges thin out:
These are places, too.
The moment in the movement of the soul
When it all seems to stop,
Seized up.
This is true, too.
Ice is, also.
And dormancy.
And I don't mean the stirring
Of seeds beneath the snow,
But the place between
And the moment before.
And I don't mean a lightning bolt,
But what it passes through.
I don't mean a dream,
But dumb sleep.
"Not a thing" is something.

After the end,
And before the beginning,
Is time, too.
Let it alone, don't try so hard.
This is God, too.
All of you is.

As a culture we are not in the habit of respecting, honoring, or even acknowledging the pause. (Culturally the most common reference to the pause was given over to Coca-Cola, which promised "The pause that refreshes." In other words, whenever there is a moment you are not busily doing something, *Eat. Drink*. And here's what we want you to eat or drink.) Women know this very well. At menopause, a time of extremely high power and shapeshifting, we are told to behave as though nothing is happening. To continue the "game" of life as if we are still girls. We are not girls. And to continue to act as though we are robs the world and the coming generations of our insights. Insights readily available to us during this particular time which is a highly significant universal moment of reflection.

I am convinced that in earlier times women during menopause drifted naturally to the edge of the village, constructed for themselves a very small hut, and with perhaps one animal for company—and one that didn't talk!—gave themselves over to a time without form, without boundaries. They were fishing in deep waters, reflecting on a lifetime of activity and calling up, without consciously attempting to do so, knowledge that would mean survival and progression of the tribe.

Until I Was Nearly Fifty

Until I was
Nearly fifty
I barely thought
Of age.

But now
As I approach
Becoming
An elder
I find I want
To give all
That I know
To youth.

Those who sit
Skeptical
With hooded
Eyes
Wondering
If there really
Is
A path ahead

& Whether
There really
Are
Elders
Upon it.

Yes. We are there
Just ahead
Of you.

The path you are on
Is full of bends
Of crooks
Potholes
Distracting noises
& Insults
Of all kinds.

The path one is on
Always is.

But there we are,
Just out of view
Looking back
Concerned
For you.

I see my dearest
Friend
At fifty-one

Her hair
Now
An even
Steel.
She blushes much
& talks
Of passion:
It cannot be
For the bourgeois
Husband
I never
Liked.

I thought life
With him
Had killed
The wild-haired girl
I knew.
But no.
There she is
There she goes.
Blushing.
Eldering.

I too talk
Stunned
Of love
Passion
Grace of mating
At last

With
My soul's
Valiant twin.

Oh Youth!

I find
I do not have it in
My heart
To let
You stumble
On this curve
With fear.

Know this:
Surprise alone
Defines this time
Of more than growth:
Of distillation
Ripeness
Enjoyment
Of being
On the vine.

I wrote this poem a few years ago, after a pause. Nor could I have written it before or during it. Before getting to the point of generosity to youth, I had to enter into, give myself over, and endure the pause.

This next poem is from that same period, but

just as this particular pause was coming to a close
and I could discern, possibly, some gifts.

Loss of Vitality

Loss of vitality
Is a sign
That
Things have gone
Wrong.

It is like
Sitting on
A sunny pier
Wondering whether
To swing
Your feet.

A time of dullness
Deadness
Sodden enthusiasm
When
This exists
At all.
Decay.

You wonder:
Was I ever "on"
Bright with life

My thoughts
Spinning out
Confident
As sunflowers?

Did I wiggle
My ears
& Jiggle my toes
From sheer
Delight?

Is the girl
Grinning fiercely
In the old photograph
Really me?

Loss of vitality
Signals emptiness
But let
Me tell you:
Depletion can be
Just the thing.

You are using
Have used
Up
The old life
The old way.

Now will rush in
The energetic,

The flexible,
The unmistakable
Knowing
That life is life
Not mood.

During the pause is the ideal time to listen to stories. But only after you have inhabited Silence for long enough to find it comfortable. Even blissful. There are stories coming to us now from every part of the earth; and they are capable of teaching us things we all used to know. For instance, driving down from the country last week—I had gone there to put in my garden, which I did—I listened to a CD called *Shamanic Navigation* by John Perkins. In it he talks about the Swa people of the Amazon. These are indigenous people who've lived in the Amazon rain forest for thousands of years. They tell us that in their society men and women are considered equal but very different. Man, they say, has a destructive nature: it is his job therefore to cut down trees when firewood or canoes are needed. His job also to hunt down and kill animals when there is need for more protein. His job to make war, when that becomes a necessity. The woman's nature is thought to be nurturing and conserving. Therefore her role is to care for the home and garden, the domesticated animals and the children. She inspires the men. But perhaps her most important duty is to tell the men when to stop.

It is the woman who says: Stop. We have enough firewood and canoes, don't cut down any more trees. Stop. We have enough meat; don't kill any more animals. Stop. This war is stupid and using up too many of our resources. *Stop.* Perkins says that when the Swa are brought to this culture they observe that it is almost completely masculine. That the men have cut down so many trees and built so many excessively tall buildings that the forest itself is dying; they have built roads without end and killed animals without number. When, ask the Swa, are the women going to say Stop?

Indeed. When are the women, and the Feminine within women and men, going to say Stop?

I used to be suicidal. I grew up in the white-supremacist, fascist South, where the life of a person of color was in danger every minute. For many years I thought of suicide on an almost daily basis. Other than this, and severe depression caused by the inevitable childhood traumas and initiations, I am not a person innately given to despair. However, it has been despairing to see the ease with which women, after over thirty intense years of Feminism, have chosen to erase their gender in language by calling each other, and themselves, "guys." *This is the kind of thing one can reflect on during a pause.* Are we saying we're content to be something most of us don't respect? *Conjure up an image of a guy.* What attributes does it have? Is that really you? Is this a label you gave yourself?

What does being called "guys" do to young women? To little girls?

Isn't the media responsible for making it "cute" to be a guy, as if that's all the Women's Movement was about, turning us into neutered men, into guys? For guys don't have *cojones*, you know. They are men, but neutered, somehow. So if you've turned in your breasts and ovaries for guyness, you've really lost out.

And does this make you remember that when we were trying to get the ERA, the Equal Rights Amendment, passed, which would have assured equal rights to women, suddenly the market and our television screens were flooded with a new dishwashing liquid called, you remember, Era. A not-so-subtle message that equal rights for women was still associated mainly with the kitchen and a sink full of dirty dishes. And it must have been in the Sixties, when women were claiming their freedom to have a good time, that the dishwashing-liquid magnates came up with a concoction called Joy.

The intuitive part of us, the deep feminine, whether in male or female, knows when we are being ridiculed, laughed at, told to forget about being women, or having a Feminine, being wild, or being free; led to sleep if not to the slaughter.

In those small areas where we do have some

control, the words coming out of our mouths, for instance:

When are we going to say Stop?

Today we are learning that the Acting President knew about al-Qaeda's plan to hijack airplanes. Long before September 11th. Knew about unusual Middle Eastern flight applicants entering the nation's flying academies. Yesterday I heard a spokeswoman for the Acting President explain that, while they knew about the possibility of a hijacking, they had no way of knowing it would not be an *ordinary* one. How were they to guess the planes would be used as bombs to demolish the World Trade Center and a wing of the Pentagon? In a pause, a moment of universal reflection, we can ponder this comment. Suppose you or I had been on one of those planes piloted by some "unusual Middle Eastern flight applicant" with only a few flights under his belt. Would we have wanted to be warned? Would we have wanted planes even to fly, until this issue had been looked into? I don't think so. Now we will have an opportunity to see the cultural resistance to dealing with the pause. We have seen it before; all our lives, actually. The rush to act. The distaste for hesitation. The absolute hatred of spending time in emptiness, what Buddhists refer to as *groundlessness*. *The Pause.*

Imagine if other members of Congress, along with our courageous Congresswoman Barbara Lee, had said WAIT. Don't give this Acting President everything he wants. Don't let him make war on anyone he chooses. Let's observe a moment of reflection. Let's give ourselves a pause. Can you imagine how much lighter our hearts would be today? How much less chocolate and junk we'd consume because we can't stop ourselves from knowing our comfort—the junk food, heated houses, spiffy new cars—is connected to severed heads, and limbs of children, lying somewhere in a ditch?

In the *Christian Science Monitor* a few months ago there was the following article:

AFGHANS SAY DIGGING CAVES FOR AL QAEDA "WAS LIKE A PICNIC"

"It started almost two months ago, and I am happy because I made a lot of money from them," says Jalad Khan, a driver who could only hope to make the 70,000 Pakistani rupees ($1,100) that al-Qaeda paid him in two to three years. "They gave us food and goat meat, and we were laughing every day. We were having a very good time—it was like a picnic."

"When we were there, they were joking with us, saying: 'We will strike the Pentagon from these mountains,' says Ahmad Wazir, an unemployed father in grime-blasted clothes. He followed that with: "I don't even know what the Pentagon is, if it is a tree or a village, or a leader."

If we pause, we can easily see that killing these men, who didn't know if the Pentagon was a tree or a village or a leader, is neither sensible nor sane. Yet I would guess that by now these men have been, thanks to our tax dollars that have purchased weapons whose only use can be for inaccurate evil, blown into pieces smaller than dust. What of the women they were laboring to support? What of the children they were trying to feed? What of their ignorance, or, more accurately, their innocence? There are millions of people living in this country who, thanks to September 11th, know where the Pentagon is, but they still have no idea what it actually does. Do you? Do you know what really went on in the Twin Towers? I don't.

Sometimes, of course, it is all simply too much. We've heard enough. We've seen too much. It is hard to bear our own human thickness. Our laziness and stupidity. Our addiction to our toys. Our comfort. Our ways of thinking and behaving. Life hears our weariness. And into it begins to pour moments of the pause. We slow down. We can't think. Our hair attracts lint. Our socks don't match. It isn't easy to see that this is a good time.

My Friend Yeshi

My friend Yeshi
One of the finest
Midwives
Anywhere
Spent a whole
Season
Toward
The middle
Of her life
Wondering
What to do
With herself.

I could not
Understand
Or even
Believe
Her quandary.

Now
Thank goodness
She is over it
Women come to her
Full
Babies drop
To her
Hand.

It is all
Just the way
It is.

Sometimes
Life seizes
Up
Nothing stirs
Nothing flows
We think:
All this time,
Climbing this
Rough tree
The rope
Attached
To
A rotten
Branch!

We think:
Why did I choose
This path
Anyway?
Nothing at
The end
But sheer cliff
& Rock-filled
Sea.

We do not know
Have no clue

What more
Might come.

It is the same
Though
With
Earth.
Every day
She makes
All she can
It is all
She knows it is all
She can possibly
Do.

And then, empty, the only
Time she is flat, She thinks: I am
Used up. It is winter all the time
Now. Nothing much to do
But self-destruct.

But then,
In the night, in
The darkness
We love so much
She lies down
Like the rest of us,
To sleep
& Angels come
As they do
To us

& Give her
Fresh dreams
(They are really always the old ones, blooming
further.)

She rises, rolls over, gives herself a couple of new
kinds of grain, a few dozen unusual flowers, a
playful spin on the spider's web called the internet.
Who knows
Where the newness to old life
Comes from?
Suddenly
It appears.

Babies are caught by hands they assumed were
always waiting.
Ink streaks
From the
Pen
Left dusty
On
The shelf.

This is the true wine of astonishment.

We are not
Over
When we think
We are.

Just this past week I've suffered from exhaustion. I got out of bed one morning determined to go to the nursery to look for heirloom tomatoes from Russia named after Paul Robeson, who sang a whole generation of rebels through some very hard times. Only to find my body was not into it. It wanted to get back into bed, lie in the sun, and sleep. Later on, a friend came and made soup and tea. And in the pause of this moment I thought of the blessing it is to have a home; to be warm and sheltered. To be cared for. I said to my friend: it is possible for everyone on earth to have this. It is not some distant fantasy, it is a reality. It is the pause that gives us this clarity, this certainty. It is our time of gathering the vision together, of reminding ourselves of what we want for ourselves and how we want the same for everyone. This is the vision most in danger of becoming extinct in our time: that what we enjoy and want for ourselves is possible for all; that this is the reality we must work toward. The pause, so brief—if only in retrospect—gives us a wonderful intuitive knowing about abundance. After all, we ourselves were empty, and now we begin to fill up again. So it is with everything.

Following is a poem about the writer's life, riddled as it is with pauses, times of incredible emptiness, times that can sometimes feel as fearful as the deepest night. And yet, with time, with maturity, and above all, with patience, one learns to dance with them.

The Writer's Life

During those times
I possess the imagination to ignore
The chaos
I live
The writer's life:
I lie in bed
Gazing out
The window.

To my right
I notice
My neighbor
Is always painting
And repainting
His house.
To my left
My other neighbor
Speaks of too much shade
Of tearing
Out
Our trees.

Sometimes
I paint
My house—
Orange and apricot,
Butterscotch & plum—
Sometimes

I speak up
To save
The trees.

The days
I like best
Have
Meditation
Lovemaking
Eating scones
With my lover
In them.
Walks on the beach
Picnics in the
Hammock
That overlooks
The sea.
Hiking in the hills
Leaning on
Our
Hiking sticks.

Writers perfect
The art
Of doing nothing
So beautifully.

We know
If there is
A butterfly

Anywhere
For miles
Around
It will come
Hover
& maybe
Land
On our head.

If there is a bird
Even flying aimless
In the next
County
It will not only
Appear
Where we are
But sing.

If there is a
Story
It will
Cough
In the middle
Of our
Lazy
Day
Only once
Maybe more
& Announce
itself.

You have completed something of major importance, your studies at CIIS. May you embrace the pause you have earned and enjoy the emptiness for all it is worth and for as long as it lasts!

Most of us believe emptiness is nothing, and we fear having nothing. Emptiness, however, is filled with possibility, filled with space. I have learned to enjoy watching my empty mind. Unlike the minds of many of my friends, my mind is often completely blank; I know it is there, but there is nothing in particular in it. My memory, for that reason, is sometimes described—by those who know me— as poor. My retrieval system slow and faulty. Having this empty mind though, has many benefits. I may not be able to recall something said twenty years or minutes ago, but I can watch the gentle arrival of something entirely new. A poem, the plot of a novel, the ending of a short story. I can "know" something in a flash, as if it simply appeared on my mind's blank screen. It is because I cherish my empty mind that I am careful what I put into it. I limit television especially, even though I think the medium of television is astonishing. I limit other things, too, like movies and public events and other people's conversations. If my mind is crowded with ideas or thoughts or plans or other people's creations there is less room for my own. And it is my own mind and journey that I wish to experience, because it is from this vantage point that I can most truly engage others.

Contemplate your mind. What is in it? What is in it that you wish were not? Is it like a clothes closet that is filled with 1980s fashion? Or is it like a busy TV show, a sitcom, where people are saying idiotic things to each other and there is canned laughter? Is it like a horror movie? Do you know how to empty your mind? Do you believe you can learn to trust a mind that isn't always speaking to you? Can you imagine a mind that feels itself part of one big mind; the mind of the Universe, waiting on instruction?

Pause for a day. Clean your mind. Sit by the ocean and let the breezes help you do this.

The River Has Its Destination

There is a message from the Elders of the Hopi Nation of Oraibi, Arizona, that speaks to this time very well. It has been circling the globe by Internet for several years and many have taken comfort from it. I read it to audiences quite often. We listen to the Hopi because they are people who have lived with Nature long enough to understand their purpose. They believe they must live simply, in a particular part of the world, and maintain specific ceremonies and prayers so that the Earth can continue to flourish. Their history contains information from times before our own when the world was destroyed. Several times. I think that because they are among the few modern peoples who seem to know and understand who they are and why they are, they are awesome teachers.

We have been telling the people that this is the Eleventh Hour
Now we must go back and tell the people this is the Hour

And there are things to be considered:

Where are you living?
What are you doing?
Are you in right relation?
Where is your water?
Know your garden.

It is time to speak your truth.

Create your community.
Be good to each other.

And do not look outside yourself for the leader.
This could be a good time!

There is a river flowing now very fast
It is so great and swift that there are those who will be afraid.
They will try to hold on to the shore.

*They will feel they are being torn apart and they
will suffer greatly.*

Know the river has its destination.

*The Elders say we must let go of the shore, and
push off and into the river, keep our eyes open, and
our head above the water.*

See who is in there with you and Celebrate.

*At this time in history, we are to take nothing
personally.
Least of all, ourselves.*

*For the moment that we do, our spiritual growth
and journey comes to a halt.*

The time of the lone wolf is over.

Gather yourselves!

*Banish the word "struggle" from your attitude and
your vocabulary.*

*All that you do now must be done in a sacred
manner
And in celebration.
"We are the ones we have been waiting for . . ."*
    —The Elders, Hopi Nation, Oraibi, Arizona

Flannery O'Conner wrote: "everything that rises, must converge." I thought of this when I saw that the Hopi elders had closed their message to the world by quoting June Jordan. This is a time when many will find, to their astonishment perhaps, that we are seeing the world through a single eye. Race will no longer matter, or sex, or gender, or orientation of any description. How we will survive will be our only concern, and who will be with us.

The time of the lone wolf, Capitalism, for instance, is indeed over. It cannot possibly sustain itself without gobbling up the world. That is what we see all around us. Women and children in Bangladesh, India, the Philippines, Haiti, Mexico, China and elsewhere in the world forced into starvation and slavery as they turn out the tennis balls and cheap sneakers for the affluent. Ancient trees leveled to make more housing while housing that could be saved and reused is torn down and communities heartlessly displaced. Mining of the earth for every saleable substance she has. Fouling of the waters that is her blood. Murdering innocents, whether people, animals or plants, in pursuit of oil. The lone wolf is the hungry ghost (in Buddhist thought) that can never get enough; whose mouth may be small but whose stomach is boundless. We cannot afford him. Even those seduced by the notion of becoming rich by playing the stock market will learn they are investing their lives in a system that feeds a vampire: the lone wolf of Profit by Any Means Necessary.

The Hopi know that Nature can stop the rampaging lone wolf. That it has done so before. That is what they are telling us. That tsunamis and hurricanes are just, one might say, the tip of the melting iceberg. That we are only beginning to comprehend how dependent on Nature we are. Hurricane Katrina, which destroyed much of the beautiful city of New Orleans and the Gulf Coast of the United States, may well be the start of a massive unraveling of everything we thought whole. And like the former Soviet Union we may find all our hopes, for a system we have believed in, dashed. What will be left?

Know the river has its destination.

I was so grateful to find this line in the message. What do you think it means? What will our destination be, if we no longer have a system that, though rotten, seems at least familiar to us? Where will we be headed if we lose everything we've known?

Sit with the Hopi message. Linger over the question "Where is your water" and the instruction to "know your garden." Consider who will be in the river with you.

What does it mean to cease using the word "struggle" and to think of celebration instead?

When I listen to this thought I hear a vast silence advancing on the world as we have known it; this vast silence is already in motion and on its way; but between its arrival and this moment the birds are singing.

5.

Crimes Against Dog

My dog Marley was named after the late music shaman, Bob Marley. I never saw or heard him while he was alive, but once I heard his music, everything about him—his voice, his trancelike, holy dancing on stage, his leonine dreadlocks— went straight to my heart. He modeled such devotion to the well-being of humanity that his caring inspired the world; I felt a more sincere individual had probably never lived. Considering his whole life a prayer, and his singing the purest offering, I wanted to say his name every day with admiration and love. Marley has grown up on his music; Bob, leaning on his guitar in a large poster on my living room wall, is regularly pointed out to her as her Spirit Dad.

Marley was born December 19, 1995. She shares a birth sign, Sagittarius, with my mother and several friends and acquaintances. At times I feel surrounded by Sages and enjoy them very much: they are fun to be with, outspoken, passionate, and won't hesitate to try new things. They also like chicken. Marley has all these qualities, though I didn't know that the morning I drove out to the breeder to look at the litter of Labrador retrievers I was told had arrived.

Crossing the Golden Gate Bridge a friend and I joked about whether I was in fact ready to settle down enough to have a dog. Who would feed it when I was distracted by work? Where would it stay while I was away on book tours? Had I lined up a reliable vet? I had no idea what would happen. I only knew this friend was about to go away on a journey of unknown length. I would be unbearably lonely for her. I needed a companion on whom to lavish my overflowing, if at times distractible, affection. I needed a dog.

On entering a place where animals are bred, my first thoughts are always about enslavement. Force. Captivity. I looked at the black and the chocolate labs who were Marley's parents and felt sad for them. They looked healthy enough, but who knew whether, left to themselves, they would choose to have litter after litter of offspring? I wondered how painful it was to part with each litter. I spoke to both parents, let them sniff my hand. Take in the quality of my being. I asked permission to look at their young. The mother moved a little away from her brood, all crawling over her blindly feeling for a teat; the father actually looked rather proud. My friend joked about offering him a cigar.

I was proud of myself, too, standing there preparing to choose. In the old days of up to several months before, if I were going to choose an animal from a litter I would have been drawn to the one that seemed the most bumbling, the most clueless, the most unamused. I saw a couple like that. But on this day, that old switch was not thrown: I realized I was sick of my attraction to the confused. My eyes moved on. They all looked much alike, to tell the truth. From a chocolate mother and a black father there were twelve puppies, six chocolate, six black. I'll never get over this. Why were there none with spots?

I asked the woman selling them, whom I tried not to have Slave Trader thoughts about. She shrugged. They never spot, she said. That's the nature of the purebred Lab.

Well, I thought. Mother. Once again doing it just any old way you like. "Mother" is my favorite name for Nature, God, All-ness.

I settled on a frisky black puppy who seemed to know where she was going—toward a plump middle teat!—and was small enough to fit in my hand. I sometimes wish I had chosen a chocolate puppy; in the Northern California summers the dust wouldn't show as much, but I think about this mostly when Marley rolls in the dirt in an effort to get cool.

After seven weeks I returned alone to pick her up, feeling bereft because my friend had already gone on the road. It didn't seem right to pay money for a living being; I would have been happier working out some sort of exchange. I paid, though, and put Marley in my colorful African market basket before stroking the faces of her wistful looking parents one last time. In the car, I placed the basket in the front seat next to me. I put on Bob Marley's *Exodus* CD and baby Marley and I sped away from Babylon.

We wound our way back through the winter countryside toward the Golden Gate Bridge and the bracing air of San Francisco. Before we had gone twenty miles Marley, now about the size of my two fists, had climbed out of the basket and into my lap. From my lap she began journeying up my stomach to my chest. By the time we approached the bridge she'd discovered my dreadlocks and began climbing them. As we rolled into the city she had climbed all the way to the back of my neck and settled herself there between my neck and the headrest. Once there she snoozed.

Of the weeks of training I remember little. Dashing down three flights of stairs in the middle of the night to let her pee outside under the stars. Sitting on a cushion in the kitchen, before dawn, her precious black body in my lap, groggily caressing her after her morning feed. Walking with her zipped up in my parka around and around the park that was opposite our house. Crossing the Golden Gate Bridge on foot, her warm body snug in my arms as I swooned into the view. She grew.

Today she is seven years old and weighs almost ninety pounds. People we encounter on walks always ask whether she's pregnant. No, I reply, she's just fat. But is she really? No matter how carefully I feed her or how often I downsize her meals, she remains large and heavy. And she loves to eat so much that when her rations are diminished she begs, which I can't stand. This is one of those areas we've had most work to do. I've settled it lately by taking her off any slimming diet whatsoever and giving her enough food so that she seems satisfied. I did this after she was diagnosed with breast cancer, had surgery, and I realized I might lose her at any time. I did not want her last days to be spent looking pleadingly at me for an extra morsel of bread. To make up for giving her more food, I resolved to walk her more.

The friend who went away never really returned. Marley and I ceased expecting to see her after about the first year. Marley was an amazing comfort to me. What is it about dogs? I think what I most appreciate in Marley is how swiftly she forgives me. Anything. Was I cool and snooty when I got up this morning? Did I neglect to greet her when I came in from a disturbing movie? Was I a little short on the foodstuffs and forgot to give her a cube of dried liver? Well. And what about that walk we didn't do and the swim we didn't take and why don't I play ball with her the way I did all last week? And who is this strange person you want me to go off with? It doesn't matter what it is, what crime against Dog I have committed, she always forgives me. She doesn't even appear to think about it. One minute she's noting my odd behavior, the next, if I make a move toward her, she's licking my hand. As if to say: Gosh, I'm so glad you're yourself again, and you're back!

$$=\bigcirc=$$

Dogs understand something I was late learning: when we are mean to anyone or any being it is because we are temporarily not ourselves. We're somebody else inhabiting these bodies we think of as us. They recognize this. Oops, I imagine Marley saying to herself, sniffing my anger, disappointment, or distraction. My mommy's not in there at the moment. I'll just wait until she gets back. I've begun to feel this way more than a little myself. Which is to say, Marley is teaching me how to be more self-forgiving. Sometimes I will say something that hurts a friend's feelings. I will be miserable and almost want to do away with myself. Then I'll think: but that wasn't really the you that protects and loves this friend so much you would never hurt them. That was a you that slipped in because you are sad and depressed about other things: the state of your love life, your health, or the fate of the planet. The you that loves your friend is back now. Welcome her home. Be gentle with her. Tell her you understand. Lick her hand.

Animals teach us to be reliable and how to serve without judgment or complaint. They depend on us for food and shelter, exercise and affection, and we commit ourselves to the discipline of never letting them down. They teach us humility.

Consider how you feel when you are cleaning up after your dog or cat. There you are, plastic baggie or scoop in hand, not knowing where the poop is going to drop, but knowing you will have to find it and remove it out of regard for others (and of course for yourself and Mother Earth). It may be firm and easy to collect, or there may be evidence of diarrhea. This is a moment of deep learning of how to *be*. Patient, compassionate, prepared. In this moment we glimpse our own possible infirmity, as we age; our own decline and mortality. We understand the importance of being able to help our aging parents or grandparents, or ill and incapacitated relatives and friends, in just this accepting way.

Cats, in particular, teach us to be ourselves, whatever the odds. A cat, except through force, will never do anything that goes against its nature. Nothing seduces it away from itself.

Contemplate ways we can strengthen our resolve to live our lives as who we really are. See the beauty, for instance, in foregoing an "important" meeting or gala event in favor of a warm fire at home and a restorative nap. What makes us purr with contentment? Find it and let it, easily, find you.

6.

This Was Not an Area of Large Plantations: Suffering Too Insignificant For the Majority to See

Dharma Talk
African American Buddhist Conference/Retreat
Spirit Rock Meditation Center, Woodacre, California
August 16, 2002

This was not an area of large plantations, since the land is hilly with some bottoms of rich soil. Whites usually had small or medium-sized farms with slaves, but one pervasive thread of "southern life" ran through Leake County history. White masters raped black slave women who bore their children, as Winson Hudson tells in her own grandmother's story. The treatment of these children varied, and sometimes they were accepted or acknowledged as relatives of the white families.

And other perversity was always looming. Percy Sanders, a descendent of an early black family in the area, recalled hearing as a child about George Slaughter, a white farmer's son by a black woman, who came to a horrible death because he "didn't keep his place." Ambushed by white men, including his own father, he was shot while riding his horse because the saddle horse was "too fine."

The story goes that when he was found, "the horse was drinking his blood."

—*Mississippi Harmony: Memoirs of a Freedom Fighter*
by Winson Hudson and Constance Curry
with a foreword by Derrick Bell

When I went to live in Mississippi in the Sixties and to work in the Civil Rights Movement, whose aim was to emancipate and empower African Americans who were still, thousands of them, treated as badly as and sometimes worse than slaves, I met Winson Hudson. She was trying to write the story of her life. I helped her, until I left Mississippi to live in New England. We sat under a tree and I wrote what she dictated. Today her story has become a book.

I begin my talk with this harrowing quote simply to ground us all in the reality of being African Americans, African-Indians, African Amerindians. We are that mixture of peoples, brought together very often and for centuries in the most intense racial confusion, hatred and violence. This horrible story, which has haunted me since I read it, is typical of the kind of psychic assault we endure, while it is exactly the kind of assault today's white majority takes no notice of, just as it took no notice two and three and one hundred years ago. This story, so chilling—The horse was drinking his blood? His own father was one of the assassins? His crime was that his horse was too "fine"?—unfortunately is one in a storehouse of such stories those of us present might hear or expect to hear, on any given day of our lives. What do we do with the shock? What do we do with the anger? The rage? What do we do with the pain?

When I read this story last month I was sitting in a federal courthouse, preparing to do jury duty. I felt ill immediately. But not as ill as I would feel an hour later upon entering the courtroom, when I was confronted with the fact that three young men of color, one Asian, two Latino, were to be tried for the murder of a policeman, whom they allegedly killed when he interrupted their burglary of a steak house. One glance at the accused trio revealed the faces of malnourished youths, barely out of their teens. The choice before the jury would be life imprisonment without parole or the death penalty. The judge, white and middle-class, well fed and well educated, seemed prepared to impose either choice.

Here were the contemporary brothers of George Slaughter.

My first version of this talk began with a poem by Bashō:

Sitting quietly
Doing nothing
Spring comes

And the grass
Grows
By itself.

I was thinking of how I found my way from the backwoods of Georgia as a young woman into the company of the finest poets. It was a route of unbelievable, serious magic. As a child my family had no money to buy books, though all of us loved to read. Because I was injured as a child and blinded in one eye, the state gave me a stipend which meant I could buy all the books I wanted. When I went north to college, my first stop after settling in my room was the bookstore, where I entered a state of ecstasy seeing before me all the books of poetry I was hungering to read. It was there in the Sarah Lawrence College bookstore that I encountered Bashō and Buson and Issa, Japanese Buddhist haiku poets who had lived centuries before. And also a book called *Zen Telegrams* by Paul Reps. We connected on the profound level of Nature. That is to say, in these poets I discovered a kindred sensibility that respected Nature itself as profound, magical, creative and intelligent. There was no hint, as there is in other poetry, that simply because humans are able to write about Nature, they are somehow, therefore, superior to it.

So this is the way I was going to start. But then I thought: it is more honest to start with the harder, more collective stuff. The stuff that makes addicts and slaves of Africans a hundred and fifty years after the Emancipation Proclamation. For I knew while sitting in that courtroom, having read the story of George Slaughter and acknowledging the young men before me as today's version of him, that the pain I was feeling is the same pain that sends our people reeling into streets and alleys looking for a "fix" to fix all that is wrong with this gruesome picture. It is the pain that undermines our every attempt to relieve ourselves of external and internalized white domination. The pain that murders our every wish to be free. It is a pain that seems unrelenting. A pain that seems to have no stopping and no end. A pain that is ultimately, insidiously, turning a generous, life-loving people into a people who no longer feel empathy for the world. We need only listen to some of our African American comedians to see that our traditional compassion for Life has turned into the most egregious cynicism.

We are being consumed by our suffering.

We are a people who have always loved life and loved the earth. We have *noticed* Earth. How responsive and alive it is. *We have appreciated it.* We have been a nation of creators and farmers who adored the Earth even when we were not permitted to own any part of it larger than our graves. And then only until a highway needed to be built or a condominium constructed on top of them.

I remember distinctly the joy I witnessed on the

*faces of my parents and grandparents as they sa-
vored the sweet odor of spring soil or the fresh
liveliness of wind.*

This compassionate, generous, life-affirming
nature of ours, that can be heard in so much of our
music, is our Buddha nature. It is how we innately
are. It is too precious to lose, even to disappointment and grief.

Looking about at the wreck and ruin of America, which all our forced, unpaid labor over five
centuries was unable to avert, we cannot help
wanting our people, who have suffered so griev-
ously and held the faith so long, to at last experience lives of freedom, lives of joy. And so those of
us chosen by Life to blaze different trails than the
ones forced on our ancestors have explored the
known universe in search of that which brings the
most peace, self-acceptance and liberation. We
have found much to inspire us in Nature. In the
sheer persistence and wonder of Creation Itself.
Much in Indigenous wisdom. Much in the popular
struggles for liberation around the world, notably
in Cuba, where the people demonstrate a generosity of spirit and an understanding and love of humankind that, given their isolation and oppression
by our country, is almost incomprehensible. We
have been strengthened by the inevitable rise of
the Feminine, brought forward so brilliantly by
women's insistence in our own time. And of course
by our own African American struggle for dignity

and freedom, which has inspired the world. In addition, many of us have discovered in the teachings of the Buddha wise, true, beautiful guidance on the treacherous path life and history set us upon.

Having said this, let me emphasize that I did not come to the study and practice of Buddhism to become a Buddhist. In fact, I am not a Buddhist. And the Buddha would not have minded this in the least. He would have been happy to hear it. He was not, himself, a Buddhist. He was the thing Itself: an enlightened being. Just as Jesus Christ was not a Christian, but a Christ, an enlightened being. The challenge for me is not to be a follower of Something but to embody it; I am willing to try for that. And this is how I understand the meaning of both the Christ and the Buddha. When the Buddha, dying, entreated his followers to "be a lamp unto your self," I understood he was willing to free his followers even from his own teachings. He had done all he could do, taught them everything he had learned. Now, their own enlightenment was up to them. He was also warning them not to claim him as the sole route to their salvation, thereby robbing themselves of responsibility for their own choices, behavior, and lives.

I came to meditation after a particularly painful divorce. Painful because I never ceased to care for the man I divorced. I married him because he was one of the best people I'd ever encountered. However, life had other plans for us both. I left my home, as the Buddha left his two thousand and five hundred years ago, to see if I could discover how I at least could be happy. If I could be happy in a land where torture of my kind was commonplace, then perhaps there was a general happiness to be found.

The person who taught me Transcendental Meditation was teaching out of the Hindu tradition and never mentioned the Buddha, the Four Noble Truths (about the fact of human suffering, its causes, the necessity to engage, endure and transform it) or the Eightfold Path, which provides a guide to moral, conscious living. What she did teach me was the deeper value of sitting quietly, doing nothing. *Breathing.* This took me back to childhood days when I did this without thinking. Days when I was aware I was not separate from the cosmos. Days when I was happy. This was actually a place where poets, time out of mind, have frequently lived. No wonder I felt at home there.

And so I laughed. The laughter bubbled up, irrepressible. I saw the path to happiness and to liberation at a glance. It was inside myself.

Now I understand that all great teachers love us. This is essentially what makes them great. I also understand that it is this love that never dies, and that, having once experienced it, we have the confidence always exhibited by well-loved humans, to continue extending this same love. The Buddha, presumably raised as a Hindu, was no doubt disheartened by its racism, i.e., the caste system that today blights the lives of one hundred and sixty million Indians. Indians who were once called "untouchables" and now call themselves *Dalits*, "those broken to pieces." They are not allowed to own land. They cannot enter the same doors, attend the schools, or drink from the same wells, as the so-called "higher" castes. Their shadow must never fall on those above them. They are brutalized and the women raped at will. *Niggers* of India, they are.

Traditionally it is taught that the Buddha discovered someone old, someone sick and someone dying, after having lived a very sheltered life, and that because of this suffering, inherent to all humankind, he struck out into the world to find a remedy. There's no mention, usually, of the horrible caste system, everywhere in place in his area, which I personally find impossible to imagine the Buddha ignoring.

I like to think of the young prince, Siddartha, observing this hypocrisy of his native religion, perhaps touching or loving an "untouchable," and deciding there had to be a better way. A higher truth. I like to think of him leaving his cushy home and delightful family, his loving wife and adorable son, and striking out into the wilderness. Searching for a way humans could rid themselves of the hideous affliction of spirit that forced division and degradation of part of the human family imposes.

Which is to say, I felt the Buddha's spirit long before I began to study his words. I felt him not as a god or as the son of a god but as a human being who looked around, as any of us might do, and said to himself: *Something here is very wrong. People are such beautiful and wondrous creations, why are they being tortured? What have they done that this should be so? How can there be an end to their suffering?*

The Buddha sat down.

Most of the representations of the Buddha show him sitting down. Sometimes he is lying down. Sometimes he is walking, though this is rare. Sometimes he is shown leaping to his feet and flinging up his arms in joy. Anyone who meditates recognizes these states. First, the sitting. The concentration on the breath. Sometimes the lying down, feeling our connection to the Mother, the great support of Earth. There is the walking, which integrates our bodies with our mind state. Then there is the feeling of exuberance when we realize we have freed ourselves. *Again.*

How does this happen?

I imagine there are people who turn to the Buddha because they've lost a lot of money. My experience, however, is that almost everyone I've met that has turned to the Buddha did so because they have suffered the end of a love affair. They have lost someone they loved. Perhaps they have lost a country, as well, or parents or siblings or some function of their bodies. But very often, people turn to the Buddha because they have been carried so deeply into their suffering by the loss of a loved one that without major help they fear they will never recover. (I actually love this about Buddhists: that though their reputation is all about suffering and meditating and being a bit low-key sexually and spiritually languid, they are in fact a band of hopeful lovers who risk their hearts in places a Methodist would rarely dare to tread.)

This is what happened to me. I had lost my own beloved. The pain of this experience seemed bottomless and endless. Enter my teacher for that moment of my life, the Buddhist nun Pema Chodron and her teachings on a set of tapes called *Awakening Compassion*. Under her guidance, far in the country away from everyone, on my own retreat of one, I learned an ancient Tibetan Buddhist meditation practice called Tonglen, along with the teachings that accompanied it, called Lojong. This involved, during meditation, learning to breathe in the pain I was feeling, not to attempt to avoid or flee it. It involved making my heart bigger and bigger just to be able to hold it all. It involved breathing out relief and happiness for myself and for everyone on Earth who was feeling as miserable as I was. I stayed at this practice for a year.

It worked.

So that today I sometimes wonder what my suffering over the loss of a loved one was really about.

And I have almost concluded that it was again the love of the Buddha reaching through two thousand and five hundred years wanting me to understand I had some control over how much suffering I endure. Wanting me to try a remedy he had found and to see for myself whether it works.

My novel *The Color Purple* was actually my Buddha novel without Buddhism. In the face of unbearable suffering following the assassinations and betrayals of the Civil Rights Movement, I too sat down upon the Earth and asked its permission to posit a different way from that in which I was raised. Just as the Buddha did, when Mara, the king of delusion, asked what gave him the right to think he could direct humankind away from the suffering they had always endured. *When Mara queried him, the Buddha touched the Earth.* This is the single most important act, to my mind, of the Buddha. Because it acknowledges where he came from. It is a humble recognition of his true heritage, his true lineage. Though Buddhist monks would spend millennia pretending all wisdom evolves from the masculine and would consequently treat Buddhist nuns abominably, the Buddha clearly placed himself in the lap of the Earth Mother and affirmed Her wisdom and Her support.

It has been enormously helpful to me to learn that the Buddha's wife and son eventually joined him in the wilderness and that she became both a follower and a teacher. There was love between them. How I wish we had a record of her thoughts. The male effort to separate Wisdom from the realm of the Feminine is not only brutal and unattractive but it will always fail, though this may take, as with Buddhism, thousands of years. This is simply because the Feminine is Wisdom; it is also the Soul. Since each and every person is born with an internal as well as an eternal Feminine, just as everyone is born with an internal and eternal Masculine, this is not a problem except for those who insist on forcing humans into gender roles. Which makes it easier for them to be controlled.

Sometimes, as African Americans, African Indians, African Amerindians, People of Color, it appears we are being removed from the planet. Fascism and Nazism, visibly on the rise in the world, have always been our experience of white supremacy in America, and this has barely let up. Plagues such as AIDS seem incredibly convenient for the forces that have enslaved and abused us over the centuries and who today are as blatant in their attempts to seize our native homelands and their resources as Columbus was five hundred years ago. Following the suffering and exhilaration of the Sixties, a pharmacopia of drugs suddenly appeared just as we were becoming used to enjoying our own minds. "Citizen Television," which keeps relentless watch over each and every home, claims the uniqueness and individuality of the majority of our children from birth. After the assassinations of Martin Luther King, Jr., Malcolm X, Che Guevara and so many other defenders of humanity, known and unknown, around the globe, we find ourselves in the year 2002 with an unelected president who came to office by disenfranchising black voters, just as was done, routinely, before Martin Luther King, Jr., and the rest of us were born. This is a major suffering for black people and must not be overlooked. I myself, on realizing what had happened, felt a soul sickness I had not experienced in decades. Those who wanted power beyond anything else—oil and the money to be made from oil (which is the Earth Mother's blood)—were contemptuous of the sacrifices generations of our ancestors made. The suffering of our people, especially of our children, with their bright, hopeful eyes, is of no significance to them. George Slaughter—the surname would have been his master/father's, and deadly accurate—was not killed, we intuit, because his "saddle horse was too fine," he was killed because *he* was too fine.

This is the bind we are in.

There is a private riddle I ask myself: Why did Europeans enslave us in Africa and take us to the United States?

The answer: Because we would not go voluntarily.

The African Americans who are aiding and

abetting the rape and pillage of Earth, helping literally to direct the bombs that fall on the innocent and the exquisite, are still another cause of our suffering. We look into their eyes and experience a great fright. They appear so familiar, and yet, somehow, we feel they are not. I do not call their names because essentially they are, as we are, energies. And they are familiar because they have been around just as long as we have. It is also necessary to acknowledge that some of those energies we find so frightening exist within ourselves.

This poem, which I think of as one of my "bitter" poems, expresses something of their position, when they can bear to acknowledge it, throughout the long centuries:

They Helped Their Own

They helped their own
They did not
Help us

We helped
Them
Help
Themselves

Beggars
That
We are.

Underneath what is sometimes glibly labeled racism or sexism or caste-ism, there lurk covetousness, envy and greed. All these human states can, through practice, be worked with and transformed. This is the good news for our oppressors, as it is for humans generally, since we all have these qualities to a degree. The equally good news for us is that we can turn our attention away from our oppressors—unless they are directly endangering us to our faces—and work on the issue of our suffering without attaching them to it. The teaching that supports that idea is this:

Suppose someone shot you with an arrow, right in the heart. Would you spend your time screaming at the archer, or even trying to locate him? Or would you try to pull the arrow out of your heart? White racism, that is to say, envy, covetousness and greed (incredible sloth and laziness in the case of enslaving others to work for you), is the arrow that has pierced our collective heart. For centuries we have tried to get the white archer even to notice where his arrow has landed; to connect himself, even for a moment, to what he has done. Maybe even to consider apologizing, which he hates to do. To make reparations, which he considers absurd.

This teaching says: enough. Screaming at the archer is a sure way to remain attached to your suffering rather than easing or eliminating it. A better way is to learn, through meditation, through study and practice, a way to free yourself from the pain of being shot, no matter who the archer might be.

There is also the incredibly useful assurance that everything is change. Everything is impermanent. The country, the laws, the Fascists and Nazis, the archer and the arrow. Our lives and their lives. *Life.* Looking about at the wreckage, it is clear to all that in enslaving us, torturing us, trying to get "ahead" on the basis of our misery, our oppressors in the past had no idea at all what they were doing. They still don't. As we practice, let this thought deeply root. From this perspective, our compassion for their ignorance seems the only just tribute to our survival.

Who or *What* knows what is really going on around here, anyway? Only the Tao, or Life or Creation or That Which Is Beyond Human Expression.

Sitting quietly.

This place of peace, of serenity and gratitude, does exist. It is available to all. In a way, this place of quiet and peacefulness could be said to be our shadow. Our deserved shadow. Our African Amerindian shadow. In European thought the shadow is rarely understood as positive, because it is dark, because it is frequently behind us, because we cannot see it; but for us, ultrasensitive to the blinding glare of racism and suffering daily the searing effects of incomprehensible behavior, *our shadow of peace*, that we so rarely see, can be thought of as welcoming shade, the shade of an internal tree. A tree that grows beside an internal river that bathes us in peace. Meditation is the path that leads to this internal glade. To share that certainty is the greatest privilege and joy.

I am grateful for the opportunity to join you in this first-ever African American Buddhist retreat in North America. Though not a Buddhist, I have found a support in the teachings of the Buddha that is beyond measure, as I have found comfort and support also in those teachings I have received from Ancient Africans and Indigenous people of my native continent and from the Earth Itself.

The teacher who has been most helpful to me, in addition to Pema Chodron, is Jack Kornfield, an extraordinary guide and human being, whose books and tapes, among them *A Path with Heart, After the Ecstasy the Laundry*, and *The Roots of Buddhist Psychology*, I would recommend to anyone who seeks a better understanding of the Enspirited Life; Sharon Saltzberg's book *Loving-Kindness, The Revolutionary Art of Happiness* has been an incomparable gift. Recently, in a book called *Knee Deep in Grace*, I discovered the teachings of the Indian female yogi, householder and mother Dipa Ma. Her instructions and observations seem endlessly potent.

I am deeply grateful to all the teachers who

came before these four that I have mentioned. Teachers from Vietnam (Thich Nhat Hahn has been a beloved teacher) Thailand, Burma, India, China and especially Tibet. I thank the Dalai Lama for allowing himself to be a symbol of good in a world that seems, at times, hopelessly tilted toward evil. I thank Martin Luther King, Jr. for the warm, brotherly touch of his hand when I was young and seeking a way to live, with dignity, in my native land in the South. And for the sound of his voice, which was so full of our experience. I thank him for loving us. If he had been able to live and teach, as the Buddha did, until the age of eighty, how different our world would be. It is such a gift to have his books and recordings of his words; and to be able to understand his death as a teaching on both the preciousness of human existence and impermanence.

And, as always, I thank the ancestors, those who have gone on and those who are always arriving. It is because our global spiritual ancestors have loved us very dearly that we today sit together practicing ways to embody peace and create a better world. I feel personally ever bathed in that love.

Let's sit for ten minutes.

Let us bring our attention to the life of our young brother, our murdered ancestor, George Slaughter. We know he was a beautiful young man, and that it was this beauty and his freedom expressing it that caused his father, *himself unfree*, to seek his death. *We can see George sitting on his stunning saddle horse.* We do not know if his half-sister, white, confused by her liking for her darker brother, gave it to him. We do not know if his mother, dark and irresistible, as so many black women are, gave it to him. We do not know if he bought it himself. All we know is that *he is sitting there, happy. And the horse, too, is happy.*

George Slaughter, an English name. We might think of Bob Marley, half-English, with his English name: perhaps George had a similar spirit. A kindred look and attitude.

May you be free
May you be happy
May you be at peace
May you be at rest
May you know we remember you

Let us bring our attention to George's mother. She who came, weeping, and picked up the shattered pieces of her child, as black mothers have done for so long.

May you be free
May you be happy
May you be at peace
May you be at rest
May you know we remember you

Let us bring our attention to George's father. He who trails the murder of his lovely boy throughout what remains of Time.

May you be free
May you be happy
May you be at peace
May you be at rest
May you know we remember you

Let us bring our attention to those who rode with the father, whose silence and whose violence caused so much suffering that continues in the world today.

May you be free
May you be happy
May you be at peace
May you be at rest
May you know we remember you

And now let us bring our attention to George's horse. With its big dark eyes. Who drank George's blood in grief after the horror of his companion's bitter death. We know by now that the other animals on the planet watch us and know us and sometimes love us. How they express that love is often mysterious.

May you be free
May you be happy

May you be at peace
May you be at rest
May you know we remember you

I cherish the study and practice of Buddhism because it is good medicine for healing us so that we may engage the work of healing our ancestors. Ancestors like George. Ancestors like George's father.

Both George and his father are our ancestors.

What heals ancestors is understanding them. And understanding as well that it is not in heaven or in hell that the ancestors are healed. *They can only be healed inside us.* Buddhist practice, sent by ancestors we didn't even know we had, has arrived, as all things do, just in time.

This is not a time to live without a practice. It is a time when all of us will need the most faithful, self-generated enthusiasm (enthusiasm: to be filled with god) in order to survive in human fashion. Whether we reach this inner state of recognized divinity through prayer, meditation, dancing, swimming, walking, feeding the hungry or enriching the impoverished is immaterial. We will be doubly bereft without some form of practice that connects us, in a caring way, to what begins to feel like a dissolving world.

In addition to contemplating the Hopi message: know your garden and where is your water, we must also ask, What is my practice? What is steering this boat that is my fragile human life?

Take some time to contemplate what sort of practice appeals to you. If you are Christian, the words and actions of Jesus are excellent guides; especially the words and actions discovered during the past century in the Gnostic Gospels and the Nag Hammadi Scrolls. If you are an animist, there is all of Existence to be inspired by. Everything has Life, everything has Spirit! Perhaps singing in the choir of your church or trance dancing with friends is a connector to the All for you. Whatever it is, now is the time to look for it, to locate it, *definitely*, and to put it to use.

7.

I Call That Man Religious

Healing the Universal Heart:
Becoming Intimate with
That Which Is Foreign

The College of Integral Studies
San Francisco, California
April 11, 2002

I call that man religious
who understands the suffering
of others.
—Gandhi

This talk was written for a convocation at the College of
Integral Studies in San Francisco, on April 11, 2002. I had
been thinking of the split between the dark and the light
mother, and how the son of the dark mother rarely has
had a voice that is listened to in the governing of the
world. It is because he speaks for the majority of mothers
and children on the planet, who are dark.

I begin my talk tonight with the words of someone
whose voice is almost completely silenced and ig-

nored by the government and media in my country: Fidel Castro Ruz, president of the Republic of Cuba. They are excerpted from a speech he gave at the International Conference on Financing and Development in Monterrey, Mexico, on March 21, 2002.

Excellencies:

Not everyone here will share my thoughts. Still, I will respectfully say what I think.

The existing world economic order constitutes a system of plundering and exploitation like no other in history. Thus, the peoples believe less and less in statements and promises.

The prestige of the international financial institutions rates less than zero.

The world economy is today a huge casino. Recent analyses indicate that for every dollar that goes into trade, over one hundred end up in speculative operations completely disconnected from the real economy. As a result of this economic order, over 75 percent of the world population lives in underdevelopment, and extreme poverty has already reached 1.2 billion people in the Third World. So, far from narrowing, the gap is widening. The revenue of the richest nations that in 1960 was thirty-seven times larger than that of the poorest is now seventy-four times larger. The situation has reached such extremes that the assets of the three wealthiest persons in the world amount to the GDP of the forty-eight poorest countries combined.

The number of people actually starving was 826 million in the year 2001. There are at the moment 854 million illiterate adults while 325 million children do not attend school. There are 2 billion people who have no access to low-cost medications and 2.4 billion lack the basic sanitation conditions. No lower than 11 million children under the age of five perish every year from preventable causes while half a million go blind for lack of vitamin A.

The life span of the population in the developed world is thirty years longer than that of people living in Sub-Saharan Africa. A true genocide!

The poor countries should not be blamed for this tragedy. They neither conquered nor plundered entire continents for centuries; they did not establish colonialism, or reestablish slavery, and modern imperialism is not of their making. Actually they have been its victims. Therefore, the main responsibility for financing their development lies with those states that, for obvious historical reasons, enjoy today the benefits of those atrocities.

The rich world should forgive these countries' foreign debt and grant them new soft credits to finance their development. The traditional offers of assistance, always scant and often ridiculous, are either inadequate or unfulfilled.

He then goes on to say:

Everything created since Bretton Woods (when the masters of the Western world gathered to decide the fate of the rest of us) should be reconsidered. A farsighted vision was then missing, thus, the privileges and interests of the most powerful prevailed. In the face of the deep present crisis, a still worse future is offered where the economic, social and ecologic tragedy of an increasingly ungovernable world would never be resolved and where the number of the poor and the starving would grow higher, as if a large part of humanity were doomed.

It is high time for statesmen and politicians to calmly reflect on this. The belief that a social and economic order that has proven to be unsustainable can be forcibly imposed is really senseless.

As I have said before, the ever-more-sophisticated weapons piling up in the arsenals of the wealthiest and the mightiest can kill the illiterate, the ill, the poor and the hungry but they cannot kill ignorance, illnesses, poverty or hunger.

It should definitely be said: "Farewell to arms."

Something must be done to save Humanity!

A better world is possible!

Thank you.

Why do millions of people the world over respect and revere this man who is consistently re-

viled by the United States? Why has our government, notably the CIA, tried to assassinate him almost more times than one can count? It is because
for over forty years he has consistently articulated,
affirmed and actively defended the aspirations of
the poor. I have myself read many of his speeches
during this period, really a lifetime, and never has
he failed to meticulously set forth the conditions
and needs of those least able to speak for themselves. This is a man who is considered such bad
news that our presidents, both elected and se-
lected, refuse to shake hands with him, or make
eye contact with him, and actually declare before
major summits, at which the world's fate is being
decided, that if Fidel Castro is present they will not
attend. This childish behavior is shameful, really,
and cowardly. And to its credit, much of the
world, though poor and illiterate, sees it for what
it is: the inability of those who profit from the
world's misery to deal with a truly religious man.*

And so I begin here, where any serious religious
exploration must: the actual situation of the peoples of the earth. We are starving, we are illiterate,
our environment is polluted almost beyond bearing, we are dying of all kinds of diseases, not just
cancer and AIDS; we are running out of water, air,
land. *The three wealthiest people of the world own
more than the GDP of forty-eight countries!* And

* To *his* credit, my fellow Georgian, former president Jimmy
Carter, visited Cuba and Fidel Castro a few weeks after this talk.

it is getting worse. However, when voices are raised to make this reality plain, and when people actually risk their lives to change the bad plan the masters of the world have laid out for us, they are in danger of being labeled "terrorists" or in other ways made to feel vulnerable, threatened, and alone.

Well, we are being disappeared anyway. We might as well make noise. How many of us gathered here have already lost lovers, children, friends, to illness that are a direct result of the way human beings, and the plants and animals they consume, are being forced to live? In my opinion what is being planned for the vast majority of humanity, assuming our so-called leaders do not blow us all up in a nuclear war, is enslavement on a global scale. Corporations, like vampires, seem to live forever, and what they crave is more and more of the earth's and the people's lifeblood. As an African-Amerindian, whose ancestors were enslaved physically for hundreds of years and many of whose people remain psychically enslaved to this day, I speak as someone returning from that condition who does not intend to experience it ever again.

In times such as these we rely more than ever on the indestructibility of the human spirit, however we define it and whatever physical or denominational robe it wears. And I will speak here of the physical body as a robe; understanding that over eons of time each of us will wear the bodies we might only have gazed upon in other lifetimes. Each of us will at some point have been white or of color, female or male, a Muslim, a Hindu, a Christian or a Jew. It is in this spirit that I salute the major recent (from five thousand years or so) religions of the world; though to be honest, I feel most of them, alpha-male-dominant to the core, have done more harm than good. I would certainly never consent to guide my own life by any religion that teaches the inferiority of women and the degradation of people of color. Or the acceptance that poverty is inevitable and husbands should control wives. That people should be stoned for any reason whatsoever. That people labeled witches should be burned. Religions that forbid women to speak in those places dedicated to the Spirit. Or even to sit or stand near anything the males consider holy. Or that violence against others, especially against anyone perceived to be "the enemy" is sanctioned by an easily irritated and wrathful God who is not moved in the least by the slaughter of pregnant women and babies. A God so jealous that all female Gods before him had to be destroyed.

But that choice is for each person to make. I do believe that when Fidel Castro Ruz doggedly speaks out for the rights of the poor, the suffering of the children, the atrocious lack of health care for the billions, that this is not simply an expression of the compassion of a devout revolutionary, but that it betrays as well the early imprinting of a radical Christianity learned by Castro in the Jesuit Catholic Church.

It has long been apparent to me that if Fidel Castro had not become a revolutionary, he would have become a priest. And perhaps, as a priest, he might have demonstrated care for the young people who looked up to him, unlike the thousands of priests who, while pretending to care for our children, have in fact voraciously and savagely taken advantage of them, sexually and otherwise; leaving broken rather than healed spirits in their wake. We will recall, sharing this moment together tonight, that for generations, not a word has been raised against these men; that it is only recently, and I believe it is thanks to the Feminist Movement, which made it safe to speak out about sexual abuse, that voices are being raised in hopes of preventing abuse of children yet to come.

My own early imprinting was likewise Christian. And though I have experienced immense sorrow over the way enforced Christianity, the white-supremacist version, wrecked and ruined my people's innate spiritual integrity, I remain a lover of Jesus, who, like Fidel Castro, Gandhi, Martin Luther King, Jr., and especially Che Guevara, never abdicated his responsibility to the suffering, the dispossessed and the poor. I see the Christ spirit in all those who cannot be bought away from their love of humanity; all those who cannot be bribed away from their love of what is compassionate and just. Even as a child, however, I found myself distracted from the demand that Jesus command the sum of my attention and devotion by the obvious goodness of my humble mother. And beyond her, the obvious goodness and magnificence of the humble, unparalleled Earth.

Now we are given to understand that human life truly did begin in Africa. Many of us knew this before, we knew it in our bones, we knew it by the way Africans, in general, and especially African mothers, have spontaneously accepted all peoples, and especially all children; a lovely quality! But what is different about today is that Science has weighed in; geneticists have spoken. The white man has lifted his voice. Each and every one of us is descended from a single woman of color, an African. A black woman who loved us enough to bother to give us birth. And look at what we have done to her. To enumerate the crimes committed against the Mother of Humanity would drive the sanest person mad. Crimes including the destruction of her worship, enslavement of her children, eradication of her image; sacking of her homeland; the raping and the murder of her daughters, over centuries, the raping and the murder of her sons. Much of the raping, pillage and murder under the blessing of the priests, and other so-called religious guides, who we now know were not merely witnesses but participants in much of the destruction and desecration.

In a recent story out of Canada, for instance, one I am sure Africans know only too well, a middle-aged Native American man committed suicide rather than endure exposure that as a child he had been sexually abused by a priest who ran the boarding school in which he had been placed in an attempt to turn him into an ersatz European. His tribe was suing the Episcopal Church for damages to the health and dignity of his people, which it had abused when they were children; but this particular Native man, while innocent of the crime committed against him by someone sworn to be concerned about his soul at least, was too ashamed to have people look at his adult body and acknowledge what had been done to him. *He was ashamed*. When in fact every elder of the church should have been on his knees asking forgiveness of him.

And after taking our mother's children away from her, after selling them into slavery, into circuses and sideshows, by the millions and by the thousands, there is the story of Sarah (Saartjie) Baartman, otherwise known as the Hottentot Venus, who was married—more accurately, enslaved—by a European man who put her in a freak show in order to exploit the visual wonder of her generous vulva, breasts and hips; and who then, after her death, prostituted her dead body and that of her dead infant; he also had her vulva cut out, preserved, and placed in the Louvre, in Paris, from which it has only recently been retrieved. To meditate on this atrocity for one hour is to change one's entire relationship to the order of the world. It is also to understand the tragedy of mistaking one's own mother's body for something completely foreign to one's self. Tragically, it is emblematic of the white world's treatment of Africa.*

In her passionately explored book *dark mother; african origins and godmothers,* Lucia Chiavola Birnbaum, of your own illustrious faculty, shares this observation about our African ancestors, so many of them artists who left thousands of vibrant paintings on cave and cliff walls:

Figures dancing, singing, playing musical instruments, engaging in initiation rituals, with body decoration and masks, characterize the art of the

---

* I am not sure where I first read the story of Saartjie Baartman. Perhaps in one of the books on African American history by J. A. Rodgers. There have been many conflicting reports about her and her remains. In one story I read years ago, her remains were in a jar on a shelf in a storeroom of the Louvre. Hence my mention of the Louvre in my talk. Having been "discovered," they were about to be sent home to southern Africa. In a current newspaper article, however, it was stated that the remains, now including not only the vulva but other "parts" of the body as well, have been stored at the Museum of Man, in Paris, and that only now—May of 2002—are they being sent back to Africa. The "husband" from earlier reports has now become a "doctor." There is no mention of a child. Saartjie Baartman belonged to the Khoisan people, who are said to closely resemble our original ancestors.

entire heterogenous african continent, according to archeologist Umberto Sansoni. Ancient art of africans south of the Sahara suggest that *they venerated their ancestors*, considered animals and all life sacred, and *that they lived without violence.* Ancient african art abounding with *fantastic creatures* evokes contemporary surrealist art . . .

When I study this art, when I engage the power and energy of its "fantastic creatures," I know I am still connected to my ancestors. Not only through my physical body, my cells and my cellular memory, my love of play and creativity, but especially through my dreams, which are also filled, at times, with visitations from "fantastic creatures" that seem to inhabit an eternal world. In this time of global upheaval and global suffering, it is to our dreams that we must turn for guidance; it is to the art inside us that hungers to be born. It is to the literature of writers who love humanity. It is to the wisdom teachings that have come down to us from those who would ease our suffering. We are an ancient, ancient people who, the majority of us, have been frightened, coerced, tricked and bribed away from the source of our greatest strength: an accurate knowledge of who we are. This nature that is nonviolent, this nature that is creative and kind, this nature that is celebratory and people- and animal-loving, this Buddha nature, if you will, is indeed our birthright, literally.

It is who we, without benefit of any imposed religion, already are.

As the Hopi say: When the grandmothers speak (and are listened to) the world will begin to heal. I say: When humankind reestablishes a feeling connection to, and a passionate love for, its dark mother—she who has been considered the least of all—the world will change overnight. For this connection, which I was fortunate enough to sense through my relationship with my actual mother, ensures a bond with the natural world that nothing can erode.

At First, It Is True, I Thought There Were Only Peaches & Wild Grapes

To my delight
I have found myself
Born
Into a garden
Of many fruits.

At first, it is true,
I thought
There were only
Peaches & wild grapes.
That watermelon
Lush, refreshing
Completed my range.

But now, Child,
I can tell you
There is such
A creature
As the wavy green
Cherimoya
The black loudsmelling
& delicious
Durian
The fleshy orange mango
& the spiky, whitehearted
Soursop.
In my garden
Imagine!
At first I thought
I could live
On blue plums
That fresh yellow pears
Might become
My sole delight.

I was naïve, Child.

Infinite is
The garden
Of many fruits.
Tasting them
I myself
Spread out
To cover
The earth.

Savoring each &
Every
One—date, fig, persimmon, passion fruit—
I am everywhere
At home.

This poem speaks to my delight at finding my way across the divides of race and gender to affirm a kinship that had been denied. In the Sixties I found it possible to love a man of European descent. Against the laws and attitudes of my country, I married him. Thirty years later I found myself deeply loving a black, black woman of African descent. Both these relationships were, in a very real sense, taboo. However, loving is nothing if it is not an education, and through the relationship with the Euro-American man I learned that all white men are not racist, are not shut down, closed off, from the life of others who appear different from themselves. The man I chose was, at that time, someone living comfortably in his fullness as a human being, without barriers between himself and a non-Eurocentric world. As a free Euro-American man, one of only a handful I have ever encountered, he was a revelation. His ability to be present and conscious among people considered "unlike" himself made it possible for me to have hope for these particular children of the ancient African common mother, the Europeans. That they have not all gone so far away from their original nature that they are irretrievable, that is to say, lost, to the concept of belonging, on equal terms, to a global, human family.

In the relationship with the black, black woman I experienced the bliss of loving my own source. I encountered the flavor of origin, a flavor expunged from much of the Western world. I understood that it is because this flavor has been largely disappeared from our lives that there is an immense suffering, especially in the Western, Eurocentric world, that shows itself as hunger. We are overweight partly because the flavor of our origins—in every respect—is off-limits to us. Hidden behind mountains of lies, misinformation, poverty, ridicule, hatred and envy and fear. Not to mention denial and guilt. We snack on an endless river of food trying to approximate something we almost remember but are at the same time afraid to recall. Absence of the original flavor, that of the black, black woman, our common mother, is the very reason people willingly endure such things as canned laughter, Muzak in elevators and pastel colors in which it is rare for anyone to look really good. (This is a joke based on the fact that black people in the South, if they were black-skinned, were told not to wear red. They were told this by their English and Irish and Scottish and French and German slave-owners. It was considered "too loud" against our vibrant darkness. We were steered instead toward more innocuous pastels. Obviously we looked great in red, just as no one on earth looks more gorgeous eating red, white and green watermelon. That was the problem.)

All the taboos set in place over the last six thousand years must be carefully brought to light, inspected in council, and probably broken, if we are to move further along our evolutionary path. They were set in place for a reason: they keep us ignorant of our true nature. I learned this once again when I was writing a novel about the practice of female genital mutilation. That the vulva was considered such an offense that it was cut off. It was taboo even to discuss it. Taboo even for the young girls who were being mutilated to cry aloud. The mirror opposite of this was the taboo in Haiti for many years against a religious ritual clearly ancient African in its origins, in which participants kiss the vulva of a dancing woman. An act described by Euro-American missionaries and others as "the obscene kiss." As if to kiss the place of our entry into this world is more obscene than to destroy it.

And why is it considered evil and obscene in a patriarchal world? Because it is a remnant of the worship of the Mother, a gesture of gratitude and blessing, that European civilization has denied and tried to wipe out.

We Have a Beautiful Mother

We have a beautiful
Mother
Her hills
Are buffaloes'
Her buffaloes
Hills.

We have a beautiful
Mother
Her oceans
Are wombs
Her wombs
Oceans.

We have a beautiful
Mother
Her teeth
The white stones
At the edge
Of the water
The summer
Grasses
Her plentiful
Hair.

We have a beautiful
Mother
Her green

Lap immense
Her brown embrace
Eternal
Her blue body
Everything
We know.

The earth mother, who stands behind the Human Mother, can be known by lying on her breast. She can be known by swimming in her oceans, or even by looking at them. She can be known by eating her collard greens and carrots. Savoring her fruits, walking through her wheat fields. She is everywhere, our Earth Mother; it is truly astonishing how often she is not seen. She may be deeply known by the ingestion of plant medicines many ancient peoples have been directed in their dreams to create, medicines that exhibit Her character of patience, loving-kindness, and healing wisdom. We are never alone; have never been alone, because Earth has always been with us. And it is to the Earth that the world will inevitably turn because really there is, ultimately, no alternative. Heaven, an idea of Earth, is not an option. When the Buddha was asked by Mara, the king of delusion, what gave him the right to teach human beings how to end suffering and to be happy, Buddha simply touched the Earth. He might also, had he known about her, have called upon his African Mother. She who lived in a time of happiness, when everything around her was considered kin. And She who was responsible, certainly, for the Buddha's curly hair, which is always a charming surprise when one studies the oldest paintings and carvings of him.

As we sit here tonight, many of us are in deep grief over the destruction of life and hope in the Middle East. Palestinians have been driven to blow themselves up in the company of their oppressors rather than live with the pain and humiliation of losing their homeland, their families, their homes and vineyards, their joy of life and their dignity. They have also, for half a century, felt misrepresented, misunderstood and abandoned by the world. Israelis, afraid and angry, have invaded their cities and massacred them without mercy. Using billions of American tax dollars to do this. At this very moment hundreds of lives, many of them children's lives, are being taken by force. There are many questions to be asked about this genocide. The Earth, we know, is impartial; she supports all alike. But the Gods involved are another story. They have sites that are so special to themselves that the killing of trespassers is not only acceptable, but ordained.

Let us affirm that Human beings do not have to remain slaves to such Gods.

In *The Color Purple*, two characters, Celie and Shug, discuss God: Shug says: *I believe God is Everything That Ever Was, Is, Or Ever Will Be.*

And that when you can feel that, and be happy that's what you feel, then you've got it. Meaning you recognize yourself as part of Everything God is. You are tied to no particular temple, wall, or rock. This was also the wisdom of Isis, Goddess of ancient Africa, who learned it, obviously, from Our Mother.

Believing this, as I do, there is no resistance to the idea that what is foreign can be known. Can be understood. Can be held in the embrace of a love that is in fact the same Love that holds the Universe. Given this Earth on which we live and grow, given its beauty and generosity, its majesty and comfort, how can one doubt that one is loved? That in fact there is an abundance, not a scarcity of love? It is all anyone ever wants, really, I believe, and it is all around us while we starve.

After many years of listening to my government's ravings against Fidel Castro and Cuba, I decided to go and visit. How foreign can these people be, I wondered, that my government thinks so little of them? I discovered a people so familiar, that without knowing the language, I felt seen, affirmed and understood. These were people of great heart, deep soul, honest intentions. They were "poor" in material goods but rich in character and resolve. They were blessed to have among them, flung around freely and at all times, more love and caring for themselves, for one another, as well as for the stranger, than I had ever seen. The God of

Love, that so many in North America had been looking for, was in Cuba. Because of hardship, suffering, human failings, some of this early beauty has been distorted or lost; still what is left of the Revolution is inspiring. What did I learn from my experience there? That I did not need to join my government in its attempt to, in Cuba, cut out our Mother's heart. After four visits, two of which afforded me the opportunity to shake hands with and even hug "the enemy," Fidel Castro, and definitely to look him in the eye, I concluded what I had already suspected: that he is my brother. Our brother. How was it possible, I wondered, that nine American presidents had failed to comprehend what I could plainly see? That they saw only the return of their previous "ownership" of Cuba as a desirable goal, and not the health and happiness of an honorable people? That they placed no value on the possibility of friendship between our two peoples simply astounds anyone who has visited Cuba and deeply grasped the importance of Cuban thinking for the coming and present crises of the planet.

A new religion of the Earth, based on the best wisdom of the past and all the information that science and genetics is bringing us, is being born. We are beginning to write our own gospels; compose our own songs of praise. (In that regard, another member of your faculty, Jennifer Berezan, is composing music that is charting our spiritual growth perfectly). We are beginning to articulate our own philosophies. To worship the Great Mystery, which is never static or dogmatic, but always evolving, ever unfolding. It is a religion in which it is a given that we share a common Earth Mother and a common Human Mother. That we are family not only because we inhabit the same Earth house but also because we share the same DNA, and through our African foremother alone, the same mitochondria.

In my novel *The Temple of My Familiar*, a "romance" * of the last five hundred thousand years, I follow the faint trail left by ancestral mothers to a time before they were human beings, when they were "fantastic creatures" such as lions. It was important to me that I create a record that felt something like the knowledge I carried in my cells, history books having failed to confirm much of what I guessed and little of what I "knew." I needed to understand and to offer a new gospel, The Gospel According to Shug. Shug Avery, unrepentant wild woman and undomesticated blues singer, appeared in my earlier novel *The Color Purple*. She epitomizes the person of our time who, through immense suffering and struggle, accepts and affirms her own self as an expression of the Great Mystery; in her Being she is a healing medicine to those around her, because in her there is

---

* The archaic meaning of "romance" is "wisdom tale."

achieved, at long last, balance, and the ability, as Virginia Woolf might have said, to consider things "in themselves;" not as other people might wish her to, but as they actually are. In other words, she is free.

The Gospel According to Shug

To bless means to help.

HELPED are those who are enemies of their own racism: they shall live in harmony with the citizens of this world, and not with those of the world of their ancestors, which has passed away, and which they shall never see again.

HELPED are those born from love; conceived in their father's tenderness and their mother's orgasm, for they shall be those—numbers of whom will be called "illegitimate"—whose spirits shall know no boundaries, even between Heaven and Earth, and whose eyes shall reveal the spark of the love that was their own creation. They shall know joy equal to their suffering and they will lead multitudes into dancing and Peace.

HELPED are those too busy living to respond when they are wrongfully attacked: on their walks they shall find mysteries so intriguing as to distract them from every blow.

HELPED are those who find something in Creation to admire each and every hour. Their days will overflow with beauty and the darkest dungeon will offer gifts.

HELPED are those who receive only to give; always in their house will be the circular energy of generosity; and in their hearts a beginning of a new age on Earth: when no keys will be needed to unlock the heart and no locks will be needed on the doors.

HELPED are those who are content to be themselves; they will never lack mystery in their lives and the joys of self-discovery will be constant.

HELPED are those who love the entire cosmos rather than their own tiny country, city, or farm; to them will be shown the unbroken web of life and the meaning of infinity.

HELPED are those who live in quietness, knowing neither brand name nor fad; they shall live every day as if in eternity, and each moment shall be as full as it is long.

HELPED are those who love others unsplit off from their faults; to them will be given clarity of vision.

HELPED are those who create anything at all, for they shall relive the thrill of their own conception, and realize a partnership in the creation of the Universe that keeps them responsible and cheerful.

HELPED are those who love the Earth, their mother, and who willingly suffer that she may not die; in their grief over her pain they will weep rivers of blood, and in their joy in her lively response to love, they will converse with trees.

HELPED are those whose every act is a prayer for harmony in the Universe, for they are the restorers of balance to our planet. To them will be given the insight that every good act done anywhere in the cosmos welcomes the life of an animal or a child.

HELPED are those who risk themselves for others' sakes; to them will be given increasing opportunities for ever greater risks. Theirs will be a vision of the world in which no one's gift is despised or lost.

HELPED are those who strive to give up their anger; their reward will be that in any confrontation their first thoughts will never be of violence or of war.

HELPED are those whose every act is a prayer for peace; on them depends the future of the world.

HELPED are those who forgive; their reward shall be forgetfulness of every evil done to them. It will be in their power, therefore, to envision the new Earth.

HELPED are those who are shown the existence of the Creator's magic in the Universe; they shall experience delight and astonishment without ceasing.

HELPED are those who laugh with a pure heart; theirs will be the company of the jolly righteous.

HELPED are those who love all the colors of all the human beings, as they love all the colors of animals and plants; none of their children, nor any of their ancestors, nor any parts of themselves, shall be hidden from them.

HELPED are those who love the lesbian, the gay, and the straight, as they love the sun, the moon, and the stars. None of their children, nor any of their ancestors, nor any parts of themselves, shall be hidden from them.

HELPED are those who love the broken and the whole; none of their children, nor any of their ancestors, nor any parts of themselves, shall be hidden from them.

HELPED are those who do not join mobs; theirs shall be the understanding that to attack in anger is to murder in confusion.

HELPED are those who find the courage to do at least one small thing each day to help the existence of another—plant, animal, river, or human being. They shall be joined by a multitude of the timid.

HELPED are those who lose their fear of death; theirs is the power to envision the future in a blade of grass.

HELPED are those who love and actively support the diversity of life; they shall be secure in their differentness.

HELPED are those who know.

Understanding that the world is engaged in ever increasing spirals of violence and suffering, I asked Spirit to give us a peace chant and mudra. I will teach it to you, if you will please stand.

When humankind writes new laws of behavior for the world, in some Time quite different from now, one of the first must be that no one will harm anyone less powerful without first visiting her or him; eating and drinking with her or him, and meeting his or her family. I am deeply disturbed by the long-distance murder of poor and defenseless people that passes for legitimate "war" in our time. It is incredibly cowardly, and I marvel that more people don't jump up and down in the streets, pointing this out. How much courage does it take to point and shoot a missile at a town you've never seen, filled with children whose voices you've never heard?

What is religion for if it is not to protect each other? To see and understand each other's nightmares and fears, worries and heartaches? Our dreams and hopes for ourselves and our offspring? If a religion's primary meaning becomes the destruction of its enemies, it has ceased to be of use in the healing of the world. It has ceased to be religious.

I am glad that I traveled to our "enemy" the Soviet Union when I was young. Deeply grateful that I have made my own connection to the Cuban people, a connection of solidarity and love I will honor always. I am happy to have met and loved actual Africans, women and men, boys and girls, so that as the world watches Africans die in the millions of IMF– and World Bank–engineered poverty and instability, I know from experience the loss we bear. I do not grieve in the abstract, but in the heart.

Think of revolutionaries and revolutions you have admired. Not just Fidel Castro or Che Guevara, Rosa Luxemburg or Martin Luther King, Jr., or Gandhi. Christ and the Buddha were also revolutionaries. Contemplate what it has meant to many of them to face relentless repression. Consider the loss of new thought, new ways of being for humanity, because of this repression.

Is there a "bogeyman" person (like Fidel Castro) or "Axis-of-Evil" country (like Iran or North Korea) you would like to know more about? Consider a visit. What will be the greatest surprise? That the people remind you very much of folks you know. That they are trying to live their lives the best way they can, just as you are. That there are only fathers and mothers and children and grandparents, like everywhere else. Ask yourself how you will feel if your government harms them.

I believe Americans are predominantly good. That they are generous and warmhearted. Kind and often passionate about freedom and justice. Any struggle for peace, freedom, love or justice I have found myself in has been thick with Americans. This is one reason foreigners have considered Americans "lucky." It has never been only our materialism they have admired, but also our spirit.

Meditate on your own view of Americans and what it means to be an American—a *North* American: a person from the US of A. This is a time to feel compassion for our country, at the same time that we may feel despair, sadness, anger or disgust. It is a country built on so many lies, it is almost impossible for it to find its way; its very foundation is murder and theft. And yet, I remember a story told at an Un-Thanksgiving celebration some years ago, on the island of Alcatraz, in the San Francisco Bay. A Native American woman from one of the East Coast tribes told of the early contact between her people and the Pilgrims. To the surprise of many in the huge circle of people gathered, she said that her people and the Pilgrims had gotten along splendidly. That the Pilgrims and her people had shared many philosophical and spiritual concepts. That the Pilgrims had loved and learned their language and had written it down, thereby preserving it. That today, because of this, she and her tribe (and I am sorry I do not recall its name) are learning their language (from the Pilgrims' transcript) for the first time in modern history.

That there might have been real peace, symbolized by the feast of Thanksgiving, between Pilgrims and Indians, had never seemed probable to me, so great was the slaughter of Native people that followed it.

How do you wish to meet new people? By sharing recipes, and cooking and eating dinners together; by learning their medicines and dances and gardening techniques, their wisdom and philosophy; by listening to the sound of their language and trying to learn it? While sharing what you have? Or do you wish to meet them via television, as they mourn the children you have killed? The farms you have destroyed? The temples and tombs you have shattered? The sacred Mother or Fatherland you have trashed?

As Americans we have a rich history of both heroes and villains. If we cultivate the compassionate understanding that even the "worst" people are undoubtedly doing the best that they know, and that this "knowing" is often sourced by ignorance, suffering and fear, we can learn from them all.

In this time, which the medieval prophet Nostradamus predicted as a period of unparalleled violence and war (lasting twenty-seven years), a time that would see much of the Earth destroyed by war, we can set our personal intention on peace, in whatever situation we find ourselves; that small contribution can be our thanks for all that we, as "lucky" Americans, have enjoyed.

8.

Now that You Are with Me Like My People
and
The Dignity of the World

Letters of Love & Hope
The Story of the Cuban Five

The story of the Cuban Five is one of courage, great sacrifice, and love. It is a story for the ages; especially for those of our people who have suffered under the implacable oppression of white American supremacy; a rule of color and power the rest of the world appears destined to experience. In September of 1998 five Cuban men, Gerardo Hernández Nordelo, Ramón Labañino Salazar, Antonio Guerrero Rodríguez, Fernando González Llort, and René González Schwerert, were arrested in Florida. Charged with espionage and other "crimes" against the United States, they were convicted in Miami, a place notorious for its hatred of the Cuban revolution, Fidel Castro, and all things relevant to the social, cultural and spiritual aspirations of the Cuban people. The five men were treated atrociously, as Cubans routinely have been and darker-skinned Cubans even more so, in prisons in the United States. Although judges were unable to define a specific "crime" the five had committed, beyond attempting to discover and alert their country of planned terrorist attacks— which Cuba has suffered for decades from Miami-based Cubans backed by the United States government—they were treated sadistically: denied the right to bail, separated from their families, and kept for seventeen months in solitary confinement in an attempt to break their bodies and their spirits. They were given ridiculously long sentences: one of them, Gerardo Hernández Nordelo, was given two life sentences, plus. And there are other horrors that the men in these pages refrain from describing out of compassion for their families and the people of Cuba who suffer intensely from their plight.

The treatment they have received is shameful. The silence around this treatment even more so. Where are the Congress members, the senators and representatives, we should be able to rely on in cases such as this? People with the courage to insist that prisoners not be subjected to torture. That their children not be denied access to them, that their wives and mothers not be driven to despair by the many failed attempts they make to see their incarcerated kin—wrongly incarcerated, in this case. Unfortunately, many of our leaders seem to view Florida's Cuban conservatives, including the assassins and terrorists among them, as People Who Vote. It appears they will endure any degree of inhumanity against any number of babies, children, old grand-aunts and nursing mothers, grandfathers and soccer players, if they can secure the collective vote from this terrifying electorate.

Fortunately, my introduction to *Letters of Love & Hope: The Story of the Cuban Five* is not about the painful failings of our leaders. Who never seem to realize how we, who vote for them, also suffer, when they do nothing; as good people, like the Cuban Five, whose behavior we can completely understand, are crucified for trying to prevent destruction of human life.

What floated up to consciousness for me as I read these letters back and forth between incarcerated fathers, sons, husbands; and wives, children, and mothers attempting desperately to reconnect, was a realization of how old this story really is. When I read these letters and poems and viewed the drawings, I was connected to those of our ancestors who first experienced the wrenching devastation of the destruction of their families. I felt in my own body the long centuries of slavery, of the systematic—and to our ancestors, insane—focus of the slave-owners on tearing families apart. How courageously so many of our ancestors must have defended, or tried to defend, this precious unit, the family. How many centuries it must have taken to almost conquer familial devotion. For some of our ancestors the voiding of familial feeling was achieved. They became zombies who learned to help their masters subdue and destroy others who were enslaved. Their descendents are those today who sell, within as well as without their families of birth, crack cocaine and other addictive drugs. They are also the allies of those in power, aiding and abetting the squashing of all rebellious, "disobedient" life.

There are fathers among the hundreds of thousands in jail in the United States, and a huge number of mothers as well. What is happening to their children, who frequently follow their parents into a lifetime of encounters with police power, humiliation, loss of contact with society, incarceration? How defenseless these children are, and how robbed of the love and guidance that should be every child's birthright.

When I was asked to write an introduction to this book I had no idea how it would speak to me. I was attending the 2004 International Book Fair in Havana; my own book *Meridian* had been translated into Spanish and presented. I flew in for the occasion and found that Cuba now has a 100-percent literacy rate. It was amazing to see the hundreds of children, mothers, fathers, grandparents, everyone it seemed, rushing to the book fair on foot. The fair itself was held in what used to be a fort. The room in which my book was presented and, afterward, a dialogue convened, was just behind what had been the office of Che Guevara during his lifetime. A bronze bust of him graces the foyer. As I was being interviewed I stroked his metal locks, amused, as I think he would have been, that so fluid a spirit had been memorialized in such a monument. To me, Che continues to have a numinousness, a radiance, that means, I think, that he will be remembered, and used as a guide, for many generations to come. His example of how to live and die certainly must be part of the nourishment that sustains *Los Cincos*, as the Cuban Five are affectionately called.

As determined as they were to bring Elián González home; that is how determined every Cuban I spoke with seemed to be on freeing the Cuban Five. There was not a single conversation that did not end on their situation, even if it started someplace else. It was Ricardo Alarcón, head of the Cuban National Assembly, who talked to me about the letters and drawings that had been made into a book and asked if I would consider introducing it. Although I support the Cuban revolution, because I also believe in free education, free health care, 100 percent literacy, and other goals and accomplishments it has achieved, I am by nature wary of leaders. Even modest, excellent ones, as Alarcón has the reputation of being. Too many disappointments. And so I was not, at the moment of being asked, overjoyed. Though I was deeply impressed by the intensity of everyone's appreciation of the five. *Los Cincos* are heroes to their people of the kind usually encountered in myth.

However, as I started reading, I began to see how important this book is for our time. The time of *so many parents in prison*. It is a primer that can be put to use immediately for the teaching of one of the most important lessons of all: how to be a father, how to be a husband, how to be a lover, *how to parent*, when something as large and compassionless as the United States government stands between you and everything you love.

> *By the time I was arrested, on September 12th, 1998, you were barely four and a half months old. The night before, your mommy had gone to work and I was taking care of you. When I finished giving you your milk you fell asleep on me and I decided to leave you there while I watched TV. When your mommy arrived, she thought you were so cute sleeping like that—sprawled over me looking contented—she couldn't resist taking a picture of us. That's the last one where we're together.*
>
> *Then they arrested me and I could not even*

kiss you goodbye. When they were taking me
out of the house handcuffed, all I could do was
look at your mommy and give her a smile,
confident and optimistic.
    René

It is this smile "confident and optimistic" that
the men struggle to beam—from prisons situated
in five separate locations in the United States—
over the heads of their children, as the distance
grows and years pass. It is a warmth, a passion, a
love, extremely moving to witness. It says something basic, I believe, about the human heart. *Until
our hearts are completely vanquished, our children will continue to hear from us.* No doubt there
will be times when the children of these men com-
plain that, because their fathers were not physically with them while they were growing up, the
imprisoned men are delinquent, and irresponsible
parents. And yet, because these few, precious documents exist, these same children will have evidence that, though out of their fathers' presence,
they were never out of their fathers' love. To be a
revolutionary means, by definition, to be willing to
sacrifice. One's comfort, one's joy, one's health and
life if necessary. But what child wants to be part of
a sacrifice? What child can understand the absence
of a parent who—in trying to save the lives of all
the citizens of his country—is missing from the
birthday party given when one is ten?

*When we were able to see each other again
you were one year old. We were under
surveillance and when you realized I was
handcuffed to the chair, you must have thought
I was a dog because you started saying "bow-
wow, bow-wow." Then your mommy tried to
make you see what was really happening. "No,
Yvette" she told you, her indignant expression
sarcastic, "your daddy isn't the dog here." In
spite of the conditions, we remained in good
spirits during the visit.*

These people, these Cubans, demonized for so long because stubbornly they choose their own way, are simply people, simply human beings. It should not be necessary to destroy them to make their country safe for McDonald's and Starbucks.

*What the Revolution meant is impossible to
explain in a single letter. Millions of people
stopped living in misery; illiteracy was
eliminated; thousands of boys and girls—six
and seven years old—were able to go to school
instead of having to work to help their families
survive; thousands of people were saved from
dying of preventable diseases; the country
preserved its resources for the benefit of its own
people and a more human society began to be
built.*

René

The Cuban love of education mirrors the passion with which African Americans have traditionally viewed knowledge and learning. My own parents, some of the poorest people in the United States, with almost no resources beyond their determination, built the first school for black children in my community. It was immediately burned to the ground by white landowners. Incredibly, they, like the Cubans, were not swayed from their course, but managed, somehow, to erect another school. Every time I think of this, and of the forty million functionally illiterate people in the United States, I wish with all my heart that North Americans had had the good fortune to have people like my own parents leading the country. What a different place it would be.

It's my role as father to always be teaching—even at a distance. So I'm sending a drawing to Lisbeth, my little one who can't read yet, with some ideas and tasks for you to read to her. I'd like you to hang this drawing over her bed: it's meant to be a serious duckling, questioning whether she's done her daily chores (the list underneath). That way, she'll always see it, so that she'll remember her daddy and at the same time remember her daily responsibilities, and the drawings and notes will give her encouragement.

Ramón

My dearest son, Gabriel Eduardo,

I don't know when your mother will give you this letter—she'll know to pick the best time. There's a reason why I haven't been able to see you for so many years. I hope that you'll forgive me for not telling you sooner, but you were too little to explain things to . . .

My hope is for you to grow up to be a good person, useful to society, loyal to a true and worthy cause. Thus, you'll need to study hard, since knowledge will help you understand and shape the world around you. The most important thing is that you be a generous person, since individualism and egotism aren't worth a thing. "The person who gives of himself grows," said Che to his children. "Above all, always be able to feel deeply any injustice committed against anyone anywhere in the world." Be honest, just, brave, and you'll always be respected. Love your country . . . and your people.

Antonio

This is a book whose beauty sinks in slowly, as the reader gradually comprehends the seriousness of what is being attempted. Nothing less than being fully present to the growth of one's children while being not only absent but locked up, far away, in small prison cells. In a place where there is ice and snow.

Little daughter, next year you'll be fifteen, and I'll try to make it the most wonderful birthday of your life. Tell me how you're planning to celebrate, what plans your mother has, all the ideas you've come up with.

Precious one, since you're becoming a young woman, I think it's a good time to talk about more mature and serious topics. Today I want to talk with you about love, but only to give you some advice . . .

For that, for my absences, because I couldn't be at Mommy's side during her pregnancy, because I couldn't see you be born, because I couldn't be there when you opened your precious eyes for the first time, or to change your diapers, or help you take your first steps or clean up your "pee-pee" and "poo," or see your first smile or hear your first words . . . for not taking care of you when you were sick or playing with you all the games fathers love to play with their children, not even being able to teach you your first vowels or read you your first book, and for the fact that my littlest barely knows me. For all that, I apologize, my beloved daughters.

But I want you to know that I had to leave because of my love for you and everyone. That wherever I have been and wherever I will be, you have been and will always be with me.

Be strong, very strong to face whatever life

*brings with a smile. Don't be afraid for me, I
am well and I am strong, especially now that
you are with me like my people and the dignity
of the world. I'll come back, never doubt that,
as soon as I can, because I miss you very much.
When I come home, we'll make up for all my
absences, and rebuild all the hopes and dreams
that have been waiting for us.*

Daddy Ramón

Like our own beloved Mumia Abu-Jamal, likewise innocent, likewise framed, also a hero by any
standard—locked down on Death Row for so
many pitiless years—these men are demonstrating
something extraordinary that must not be missed
by the rest of us: that continuing to love with depth
and tenderness honors revolution at its highest
success.

What is your relationship to the prison-industrial
complex? Do you, knowingly, have one? Are your
wonderfully inexpensive clothes, tires, toys, made
by people who are imprisoned for petty "crimes"
you yourself might have committed, but because
you are protected by status or wealth you feel im-
pervious to injustice?

I have worn a "Free Mumia" button for at least

a decade. People I like a lot ask me: Who or what is a Mumia? I see in their eyes a chilling innocence. Not to know anything about the United States' political prisoners is to miss important information about the land we call home.

Sit with the thought that our prisons are bursting with inmates, many of them women and children. That African Americans make up 44 percent of the prison population but are only 12 percent of the population of the country.

Consider what Jesus meant when he said "What is done to the least of these is done also to me."

What is our responsibility to Justice in a society that privatizes the building of prisons and dreams up reasons to build more and ways to keep them full?

9.

Metta to Muriel and Other Marvels: A Poet's Experience of Meditation

At a recent weeklong silent retreat I had the insight that if I had not divorced my very admirable husband and suffered horribly the irrevocable loss of his friendship, I might never have discovered meditation. Although the ancient Chinese alerted us to the fact that one house move is equal to three fires, no one had told me how difficult it would be to separate from someone I loved deeply but did not wish to live with anymore.

I came to meditation, then, as most people do: out of intensity of pain. Loss, confusion, sadness. Anxiety attacks. Depression. Suicidal inclinations. Insomnia. A good friend told me about it, and I almost didn't listen because I knew she was having an affair with the teacher of meditation she so heartily endorsed. Still, the pain was unresponsive to everything else I tried.

I remember sitting on my cushion thinking this will never work, and then gradually, later in the night, realizing that I wasn't quite so jumpy, and that mornings no longer made me want to draw the covers over my head. I could listen to the radio, to music at least—which my soul had banned—almost normally, and in general it began to seem as if my inner vision had cleared.

After a week of lessons there was a ceremony announcing my mastery of technique. To my surprise at this event, during meditation, I felt myself drop into a completely different internal space. A space filled with the purest quiet, the most radiant peacefulness. I started to giggle and then to laugh. I knew I'd gotten it. And what I'd gotten was that meditation took me back to my favorite place in childhood: gazing out into the landscape, merging with it and disappearing.

This is not what meditation is for everyone, of course. During a public dialogue with a master Buddhist teacher, Pema Chodron, I mentioned the joy of the "disappearing act." I said that it was probably what being dead would be like, and that you'd be surprised how much you enjoyed it. She said for her it was just the opposite. She felt, while meditating, totally present, aware of everything around her. Actually this has become more of what meditation is like for me as well, and though the Buddha teaches us not to cling, and especially not to cling to transitory states of consciousness, I do sometimes miss those brief moments of ego-absent bliss.

As I settled into meditation nearly twenty years ago, there in my two-and-a-half-room apartment, having given up the eleven-room house I'd lived in along with the admirable husband, I was surprised to find how many and how varied one's transitory states can be. There were sittings that were amazingly sexual, for instance, as if my *kundalini* energy had been waiting for me to sit down.

There were times when I wept copiously as old sorrows from the past put in their final bids for my undivided attention. There were times of pure joy, as I felt the lightness of heart that comes from knowing you've found something truly reliable and helpful.

Meditation has been a loyal friend to me. It has helped me write my books. I could not have written *Possessing the Secret of Joy* without it; writing *The Temple of My Familiar* (my "great vision" novel of how the world got to be the way it is) would have been impossible. *The Color Purple* owes much of its humor and playfulness to the equanimity of my mind as I committed myself to a routine, daily practice.

It has helped me raise my child. Without it the challenge of being a single parent would have overcome me. It has made many losses bearable. Not just that of my former friend, the man I married, but the loss of other loved ones, communities, cultures, species, worlds in this time we live in, in which to honor our broken hearts, by peering quietly and regularly into the expanded opening, is to nurture a beginning to the re-creation of hope. And the magic of meditation remains.

It is a time when ancestors sometimes appear.

At the same silent retreat at which I understood how my early loss had led to a cherished gain, I became deeply engaged in *metta*, "loving-kindness" meditation. We were being guided to send metta to a loved one, a benefactor, a neutral person and a difficult person. The difficult person is always rather amusing to choose, because the moment you do so, you begin to see how much that person resembles yourself.

But it was the benefactor that proved momentarily difficult. The metta that one sends is: "May you be happy. May you be safe. May you be peaceful. May you have ease of well being." The trouble was, I had so many benefactors to choose from.

I thought of two of my teachers, Howard Zinn and Staughton Lynd, historians and activists, who, while I was in college, taught me with the caring and patience of older brothers. I thought of Charles Merrill, a man who has made good use of the money his father (of Merrill Lynch) left him, by giving a lot of it away; some of it to me when I was a poor student without even a pair of warm shoes. I thought of Marian Wright Edelman (of the Children's Defense Fund), whose work helping children benefits our whole society.

For a while all four of these people merged. But then just behind them rose the face of my poetry teacher, the woman I always said, behind her back of course, dressed like Henry VIII. Because she wore huge Russian-inspired hats made of fur, substantial boots and black-and-green clocked tights. Muriel Rukeyser. Poet, rebel, visionary, life force.

It was the clearest I had been able to see her since I'd known her at Sarah Lawrence, and she looked nothing like she had—pale and weakened—in the years, much later, before she died. She looked ruddy and mirthful, and she was laughing. At Sarah Lawrence she had submitted my very first poems to the *New Yorker*. They were rejected; and just up from rural Georgia, I had no idea what the *New Yorker* was. But that she'd done it, instantly, on reading them, endeared her to me.

Later she found an agent for me and introduced me to one of the great loves of my life, Langston Hughes. She would be the godmother to my first book of poems, as Hughes would be godfather to my first published short story.

These two are prime examples of "the American race" that, in America, is always behind us and also always coming into being.

With much gratitude and emotion in my heart I began to send metta to Muriel.

May you be happy, I said.
I am happy, she said.
May you be safe, I said.
I am safe, she said.
May you be peaceful, I said.
I am peaceful, she said.
May you have ease of well-being, I said.
I have ease of well-being, she said.
May you be joyful, I added, just to be sure to cover
everything.
I am joyful, she said. As if to say:
I'm in heaven, of course I'm joyful.

Heaven. Now there's a thought. Nothing has ever been able, ultimately, to convince me we live anywhere else. And that heaven, more a verb than a noun, more a condition than a place, is about leading with the heart in whatever broken or ragged state it's in, stumbling forward in faith until, from time to time, we miraculously find our way. Our way to forgiveness, our way to letting go, our way to understanding, compassion and peace.

It is laughter, I think, that bubbles up at last and says, "Ho, I think we are there." And that *there* is always here.

That teachers are so often poorly paid and little appreciated is a crime against humanity. Where would we be, as a world, without those who perceive our ignorance and seek to eliminate it? We can see what has happened in many parts of the world where knowledge is kept secret from the people, especially from women and female children. Interestingly, knowledge kept secret ceases to be knowledge; it becomes dogma and superstition. Knowledge actually requires sharing in order to exist.

I have deeply loved all of my teachers, except one, a distant cousin, who frequently left us locked out of the school building on very cold days. When she finally arrived she reluctantly opened the door for her poor, shabbily clad students, many of whom went the entire day on a Coca-Cola and a bag of peanuts, and ordered someone to start up a fire; she would then sit at the head of the class glowering at us, as she nibbled through a box of prunes. But even this behavior taught me something useful: that children learn best when they are warm, well-fed, and suitably dressed, and when they are seen and loved; and that is what we must insist upon across the planet.

It is within our power to do this.

Was there a special teacher in your life who taught you more than history or literature or science, but also how to live and to think and to relate to others with compassion?

If so, consider sending metta to her or him:

May you be happy
May you be well

May you be peaceful
May you know joy
May you also know
Your student
Of so long ago
Gratefully
Remembers
You.

10.

How It Feels to Know Someone Died for You: Living with the Voice of the Beloved

Talk at UC Santa Cruz, Early Nineties

I want to talk to you about grief.

When Martin Luther King, Jr., died I was living with my husband, a white Jewish civil rights lawyer, in one of the most repressive places on the face of the Earth: the state of Mississippi. My sister once said that she was so afraid of the state of Mississippi that she didn't even want me to fly over it. My whole family thought I was crazy to try to live there. To live there, also, with a white man; my marriage to him, according to the laws of the state of Mississippi, illegal. And I don't believe my sister has flown over the state of Mississippi, or landed in it, to this day. However, my husband and I were there to change it. To make it a place that black people, who so deeply love the South, the seasons and the sun, could truthfully call home.

I was pregnant when the news of King's assassination reached us. It had been his voice that urged both of us, at separate times, to return to the South; to challenge the apartheid of Mississippi. If not for his voice, pointing out a duty it might have been safer to ignore, we might not have found each other; not to mention a large part of our life's work. Determined to follow Martin to the end, we traveled to Atlanta for the funeral. We walked behind his mule-drawn coffin for many miles. I lost the child.

How much can two people weep? It is hard to know because we were so not alone among those who were weeping all around us.

We remained in Mississippi for several years after King's death, yet for me the period following his passing represented a time of disbelief; of incredible loss; of unspeakable sorrow. Only in the South, I still believe, was he mourned as deeply as he deserved. Because as Southern-born people of color, we understood what a gift his life had offered us. His shining fearlessness. Only in the South did so many of us retreat into so profound a sorrow as to appear to have been struck dumb. I could not bear to hear his voice for a very long time.

And yet, there was a miracle too. Again, especially among black Southerners. Even in our deepest sorrow, the daily palpable ache of missing him, which never seemed to soften or to go away, we discovered a tender, radiant certainty that made some wretched, bewildered, stunned and stupefied part of us begin, almost, to smile. We knew, never not to know, that he had died for us. We knew we had been seen, held precious and dear beyond pain or price. Or sacrifice. We knew we had been completely loved. I firmly believe there is no wholeness for a people, no promised land in view, until this happens. A challenging thought. His offering of himself, in love and faith, was a forerunner of the promised land he would, at the end of his life, offer us.

And yet, there were contradictions: In my novel *Meridian*, which I wrote while living in Mississippi, being part of the Movement for black liberation and also relentlessly observing it, there is a chapter called "Free at Last: A Day in April, 1968." In it the heroine, Meridian Hill, a poor woman, attends, as I did, Martin Luther King's funeral in Atlanta.

Long before downtown Atlanta was awake, she was there beside the church, her back against a stone. Like the poor around her, with their meager fires in braziers against the April chill, she had brought fried chicken wrapped in foil and now ate it slowly as she waited for the sun. The nearby families told their children stories about the old

166

days before black people marched, before black people voted, before they could allow their anger or even their exhaustion to show. There were stories, too, of Southern hunts for coons and 'possums among the red Georgia hills, and myths of strong women and men, Indian and black, who knew the secret places of the land and refused to be pried from them. As always they were dressed in their very Sunday best, and were resigned; on their arms the black bands of crêpe paper might have been made of iron.

They were there when the crowd began to swell, early in the morning. Making room, giving up their spots around the entrance to the church, yet still pressing somehow forward, with their tired necks extended, to see, just for a moment, just for a glimpse, the filled coffin.

They were there when the limousines began to arrive, and there when the family, wounded, crept up the steps, and there when the senators running for President flashed by, and there when the horde of clergy in their outdone rage stomped by, and there when the movie stars glided, as if slowly blown, into the church, and there when all these pretended not to see the pitiable crowd of nobodies who hungered to be nearer, who stood outside throughout the funeral service (piped out to them like scratchy Muzak) and shuffled their feet in their too-tight shoes, and cleared their throats repeatedly against their tears and all the same hopelessly cried.

Later, following the casket on its mule-drawn cart, they began to sing a song the dead man had loved. "I come to the gar-den a-lone . . . While the dew is still on the ro-ses . . ." Such an old favorite! And neutral. The dignitaries who had not already slipped away—and now cursed the four-mile walk behind the great dead man—opened their mouths in genial mime. Ahead of Meridian a man paraded a small white poodle on a leash. The man was black, and a smiler. As he looked about him a tooth encased in patterned gold sparkled in his mouth. On the dog's back a purple placard with white lettering proclaimed "I have a dream."

Then she noticed it: As they walked, people began to engage each other in loud, even ringing, conversation. They inquired about each other's jobs. They asked after each other's families. They conversed about the weather. And everywhere the call for Coca-Colas, for food, rang out. Popcorn appeared, and along their route hot-dog stands sprouted their broad, multicolored umbrellas. The sun came from behind the clouds, and the mourners removed their coats and loosened girdles and ties. Those who had never known it anyway dropped the favorite song, and there was a feeling of relief in the air, of liberation, that was repulsive.

Meridian turned, in shame, as if to the dead man himself.

"It's a black characteristic, man," a skinny black boy tapping on an imaginary drum was saying. "We don't go on over death the way whiteys do." He was speaking to a white couple who hung on guiltily to every word.

Behind her a black woman was laughing, laughing, as if all her cares, at last, had flown away.

Martin Luther King, Jr., had asked us to do something really hard. Many people felt he had asked us to do something impossible. He had asked us to embrace nonviolence as a way of life. When he died by the gun, for many, many people, in the Movement and out of it, there was a feeling of release. We can't do it, many felt; we can't live as nonviolently as Martin Luther King, Jr., did (and once again the white man—in the person of King's assassin—has demonstrated why).

It was shocking to feel this. At the same time, it was completely understandable. I went through a period of being afflicted by horrible fantasies: of blowing up terrorists. Members of the Ku Klux Klan and the White Citizens Councils, racist fanatics of all kinds who daily tormented and harassed us. And of course blowing myself up with them, since, as a pacifist, and a deep believer in nonviolence, I could never imagine murdering another without also murdering myself. This was a particularly bleak and dreary dark night of the soul. I survived it partly because of King's example.

Our communities did erupt in violence, many of them; several went up in flames. The youth, especially, could no longer bear to consider nonviolence an option for changing the world. Guns flooded our neighborhoods. Accompanied by the handiest painkiller, illegal drugs. *Because it was pain; all of it.* The rage, the laughter, the feeling of being relieved of a burden too noble for mere persecuted humans to bear. And underneath everything, the longing for the presence of the Beloved. *Deeply missing him.* The one who loved us and saw us and stayed with us, knowing he would not survive his blatant love for us; not survive his vibrant, dancing life.

There was a rumor, when I was at Spelman College, which is across the street from Morehouse, Martin Luther King, Jr.'s school, that he was a terrific dancer. Some of the Movement's tacticians, who also didn't want us to know a few of our leaders were gay, didn't want us to talk about this; I think because he was a preacher. This made it all the more amusing later, when the planet discovered that J. Edgar Hoover, the gay head of the FBI, audiotaped him doing more than dancing, and apparently having an exhilarating time. I met him during that period of flying rumors. I was sent by my instructor in speech class to attend one of King's lectures and to write, literally, about how he spoke. We were warned to write nothing of his politics. That's the kind of school Spelman was at the time, even though students were risking arrest and being arrested, eagerly listening to Martin's every word, every day. After his talk he shook hands with each of us. He had been brilliant. Mesmerizing. But since I couldn't write about what he said, I wrote about what he wore. A really neat gray suit. And talked about his accent, which I thought was pretty broad, pretty funny. Moving beyond belief, though, was the message of his speech: that by freeing ourselves nonviolently we could also free our oppressor. Though it was an impassioned speech, he didn't seem particularly attached to it. This detachment was characteristic of him, I was to observe in years to come. An old soul, he already appeared to have the overview of an ancestor. His was a deep love for humanity, and it was wonderfully impersonal. Curiously, this meant that his speeches were unfailingly electrifying. Bringing his audiences to tears and laughter and spontaneous delight in the truth of his words, no matter how bleak.

He was someone who, in a sense, was living, consciously, toward his death.

Which is how we black Southerners felt. Martin Luther King, Jr., was not the only one who thought he wouldn't survive. Most of us thought he would be taken from us sooner. And yet, when he was no longer with us, knowing we shared this awareness with him, that he had known too, hardly made the loss of him easier to bear.

He feared no man, he said. He had been to the mountaintop, seen the promised land. He might not get there with us, he said. But we, as a people, would someday get to the promised land. What did this mean? Americans, and African Americans too, can be very materialistic. There are those who believe that because we can eat anywhere, sleep anywhere, buy houses and even airplanes almost anywhere, we have arrived at the promised land. Or, to be more accurate, *they've* arrived. Because there is still the huge problem of homeless people, sick and out-of-work people, the continued drugging of our youth in communities across the nation, plus the 1.2 million African American men in prison. Someone else has confessed to the murder for which Mumia Abu-Jamal has been on death row for over twenty years; Jamal is still behind bars. This is more the land promised by Bull Connor and George Wallace, Richard Nixon, Ronald Reagan and George Bush, than the promised land seen by Martin Luther King.

The promised land that King saw was the country of Freedom and Justice. In his speeches he says this many times. How are we to get there?

Just a few days ago I visited Ground Zero in New York City. The people have done such an amazing, loving job of cleaning up the wreckage that it is difficult to imagine all the lives lost there. And yet the people remember. They come, write messages, leave notes. Flowers. Some of the faces of those lost on that day seem to me especially beautiful. Peace-loving. I cannot imagine they would wish their own fate on anyone else.

War will never make us safe. The only way to end it is by stopping. That is the power we have as a nation; as the most powerful nation, militarily, on Earth. Imagine what that would feel like to the world. If we said, instead of bombing small children, donkeys and chickens that never heard of us: We could blow you to bits, we could pulverize you. But we won't. In fact, we are so strong that we are not afraid to listen to you. What is it you want to tell us that you thought we could not hear unless you went for our mommies and daddies, small children—five thousand of them left without a parent, in New York City—our donkeys and our chickens? Only if we can stop the terrorism in our own hearts will be we able to stop terrorism in the world.

Remember who we are. We are a people for whom someone has died. We are a people who know what it means to have been seen, claimed, and beloved.

Thousands of feet
Below you
There is a small
Boy running from
Your bombs.

If he were
To show up
At your mother's
House
On a green

Sea island
Off the coast
Of Georgia

He'd be invited in
For dinner

Now, driven,
You have
Shattered
His bones.

He lies steaming
In the desert
In fifty or sixty
Or maybe one hundred
Oily, slimy
Bits.

If you survive
& return
To your Island
Home
& your mother's
Gracious
Table

Where the cup
Of loving-kindness
Overflows

The brim
&
From which
No one
In memory
Was ever
Turned

Gather yourself.
Set a place
For him.

We are a people—African Americans, Amerindians—who have always welcomed the stranger. Perhaps this is the most enduring definition of "indigenous." Of the truly civilized, or, a word I prefer, cultured. It has cost us. And yet, it is a surer path to the promised land of Freedom and Justice, than is war.

Not Children

War is no
Creative response
No matter
The ignorant
Provocation
No more
Than taking

A hatchet
To your
Stepfather's
Head
Is
Not to mention
Your husband's.

It is something
Pathetic
A cowardly servant
To base
Emotions
Too embarrassing
To be spread out
Across the
Destitute
Globe.

The only thing
We need
Absolutely
To leave
Behind
Crying
Lonely
In
The dust.

Remember who we are. Precious. Radiant. Seen. Beloved. And if they say your self-regard and love of Earth and humanity is unpatriotic and a threat to the Fatherland—America has become almost entirely masculine; have you noticed?—offer this poem:

Patriot

If you
Want to show
Your love
For Americans
Love
Americans
Smile
When you see
One
Flowerlike
His
Turban
Rosepink.

Rejoice
At the
Eagle feather
In a grandfather's
Braid.

If a sister
Bus rider's hair
Is

Especially
Nappy,
A miracle
In itself,
Praise
It.

How can there be
Homeless
In a land
So crammed
With houses
&
Young children
Sold
As sex snacks
Causing our thoughts
To flinch &
Snag?

Love your country
By loving
Americans.

Love Americans.
Salute the Soul
& the Body
Of who we
Spectacularly
&

Sometimes
Pitifully are.

Love us. We are
The flag.

The sixteenth-century mystic and prophet Nostradamus foresaw a future, four hundred years ago, that had someone like Osama bin Laden—a prince from the East bent on our destruction as a country—in it. And Cheney and Bush. And us, the masses of earthlings, trying with a bit of dignity and luck to get by. He saw the world engaged in war, including nuclear, for twenty-seven years. According to him we are in for a period of incredible destruction. Because of famine and war, he said, people would begin to eat each other. I think of this when I hear reports about the people our military is bombing in Afghanistan: that they are starving and cold, that they are eating cakes made of grass. September 11th has demonstrated that America is not immune to the suffering of the world. Karma means we will not avoid reaping whatever we sow.

It may well be too late. Martin Luther King, Jr., said that these two words are perhaps the saddest in human language: *Too late.* And yet, like him, I do not entirely despair. I like to think of the last night of his life: he'd been depressed, ill with a cold. He felt he couldn't speak to a crowd who had assembled to hear him. He sent someone else, his friend and colleague, the Reverend Abernathy, in his place. But Martin was sent for; the crowd wanted to hear him, no matter how sick he was feeling, and he went. It was that night that he told the world what he had seen: a promised land of Freedom and Justice for our people. After that speech, his cold seemed to disappear, his spirits brightened. One of the last acts of nonviolence Martin Luther King, Jr., engaged in was a pillow fight, back at the hotel, with his associates. I love this image of him. Laughing, throwing pillows.

Let us take a moment to imagine him doing this. Let us take a moment to smile.

Most of the photographs of King show someone very solemn, very serious. But he had a merry laugh and a beaming smile. He liked to hear jokes and enjoyed his own. I think he was more like the Buddha than like the Christ image that has been handed down to us.

Nostradamus said that after the destruction of this world, there would again be peace, everywhere, and that it would last a thousand years. I offer his words not necessarily for belief, because who among us knows the future? *But for contemplation.* If we must fight the poor around the world, let it be with pillows filled with food and blankets, houses, donkeys and chickens, heating fuel and real cakes made of butter and flour and eggs and chocolate. We can easily afford this. If the war in Afghanistan and Iraq cost us thirty-five million dollars a day, we could feed and house everyone on Earth who needs it for far less. We could even throw in violins and bicycles. Generosity toward those less fortunate is the way of the future, if a future exists. Who are we, blessed with so much, to be stingy?

Remember who we are. We are the people seen and loved. All of us. As you know, Martin Luther King, Jr., never left anyone outside his heart. Not even those who jailed and tortured him. We are people worthy of generosity, passionate advocacy, abiding loyalty and love. We are rich enough to offer these things to others.

We have only spirit, of which Martin is such a radiant part, to guide us. But that is as it should be. *Spirit is Our Country* because it is ultimately our only home. Let this awareness take some of the fear out of us.

Here are two more poems to help us on our way into what will no doubt be a particularly dark and scary time.

When We Let Spirit Lead Us

When we let Spirit
Lead us
It is impossible
To know

Where
We are being led.
All we know
All we can believe
All we can hope
Is that
We are going
Home
That wherever
Spirit
Takes us
Is where
We
Live.

Remember:

Nothing is ever lost
It is only
Misplaced
If we look
We can find
It
Again
Human
Kindness.

11.

The Glimpse of Life
Beyond the Words

On Censorship and Freedom of Speech

Along with her Pulitzer Prize and American Book Award, Alice Walker has the honor of being one of the most censored writers in American Literature. Like Mark Twain, John Steinbeck, Madeleine L'Engle, and J. D. Salinger, Walker has been the subject of so much controversy that too often the artistry of her work has been lost in the politics of the moment.

—Alice Walker Banned
from the introduction by Patricia Holt,
editor of the *San Francisco Chronicle* Book Review

The first time I read Patricia Holt's introduction to *Alice Walker Banned*, a small book on censorship composed and edited by her in conjunction with the publishers of Aunt Lute Books, I was delighted to see her idea that certain forms of censorship can be seen as honoring the writer. I agree. I was content to be in the company, especially, of J. D. Salinger and Mark Twain, whose banned works I studied in college. Twain, in particular, on religious matters. It is the writer's duty, it seems to me, to question all establishment Gods, and it is a pleasure to stand with writers, throughout history, who have done so.

My other response to Holt's words was amazement. How did it happen that I should be one of the censored? One of the banned? And why has controversy about my work been so consistent that whenever I publish a novel I am tempted to attach a note to the reader warning that the book might be too much (or too something) for them? And certainly for their children, who I in no way wish to distress. Puzzled, I have asked my friends: Is it character? Is it genes?

I was born to parents who worked a farm and operated a large dairy for the landowner on what remained of a Southern plantation. They were the most law-abiding, clean-living and -thinking people I have ever known. The word "damn" was never spoken in our house. "Darn" was the only expletive I ever heard from my father, and then only when he'd accidentally hurt himself. My mother would never even say that. "Doodoo" was the common word for feces. There was virtually no mention of sex, especially around young girls. I was in college before I actually heard someone say "fuck." I was shocked.

Naturally, then, when *The Color Purple* was published my mother had a hard time with the opening pages, in which a nearly illiterate, traumatized teenager writes anguished letters to God using words that, to anyone unused to hearing them, were likely to cause offense. She was joined in her resistance to the book by many others who would read no further than she did, and who, furthermore, had the power to remove the book from school curricula and public libraries.

After Steven Spielberg filmed *The Color Purple*, my mother was able to see the story beyond the "bad" words, and to see glimpses of her own unsung mother's life. She saw the love with which the book is infused—my worldly brothers helping her grasp the possibility that not everyone possessed so lofty a mind, or pure a tongue, as she—and was reconciled to the reality that people express themselves using the words they know. And that my main character's voice, to do justice to her condition, as a poor, abused young woman in the turn-of-the-century South, had to be fairly crude.

I have come to understand, after years of controversy over my work, censorship of it, and banning, that it is "the glimpse of life beyond the words" that those who censor writers are seeking to blot out. Why else would my essay about a lonely horse "Am I Blue" be considered "anti–meat-eating" and therefore unacceptable reading matter for tenth graders, or a short story "Roselily," about a Christian woman marrying a Muslim man, be banned from a California school test because it was considered antireligious?

The freedom to speak and to write about life as

one knows or imagines it is a right that most Americans take for granted. It is that basic, and that precious. Even after all these years, nearly thirty, of writing that has engendered controversy, I am still undaunted in the face of possible condemnation and censorship. My country's gift to me. I continue to write the stories I believe to be spiritually authentic, creatively true. Stories that are medicine—sometimes bitter, but also sweet—for myself and for the tribe.

I also see banning and censorship as attempts to avoid the pain of encountering subjects that frighten or hurt. I comprehend this reaction and feel compassion for it. I have felt sadness but not much anger over repeated attempts to suppress my work. However, in order for understanding among peoples to evolve, we must continue to learn to sit with one another's truths, which to me is the real meaning of the First Amendment.

Having said that, however, let me speak at least briefly, about when, and how, censorship hurts. When I published my third novel, *The Color Purple*, and later when it became a movie, I was harshly criticized and often brutally attacked—in print and also at town-hall meetings across the country. Because I had written a novel about domestic violence and child abuse I was accused of "airing dirty laundry" that would be used against black people, especially against black men. The behavior I explored, in an attempt to bring it to light and to healing, was often said not to exist. That my vision of what I was seeing was my own fault; that I was incapable of seeing clearly. For years this battle raged within the black community. And I used to wonder, as I went about my life outside the debate, about its impact on children, black children especially, who were suffering exactly the violence and abuse I had written about. I knew that many of the young boys were learning from their elders that a black woman writer had deliberately lied about them, which must have been perplexing since many had experienced in their own lives, or seen in the lives of their friends and families, precisely the behavior I had written about. What was the impact on these young men of experiencing blatant denial of what they knew? How did this denial of reality later play into the widespread and inexplicable misogyny that followed? So that within two decades of having affirmed black women as "Mothers of the Nation" the most common descriptions of a black woman in many communities were "bitch" and "ho." The culmination of this hatred of women was exposed recently at the 2006 Academy Awards. The song that won as most original new soundtrack was "It's Hard Out Here For a Pimp." No compassion for the "ho" standing on street corners, barely dressed in the freezing cold, often hungry, trying to support fatherless children, and required to "go down" on countless unwashed men who might abuse her further if they are not satisfied. Not surprisingly, with the devaluation of the Feminine in our communities has come an unimaginable increase in violence. Violence that endangers and touches everyone.

I received many condemnatory letters regarding *The Color Purple*, as well as for *Possessing the Secret of Joy*. In one, an African man wrote that there was a saying in his tribe that "to tell the truth hurts the people." This was by far the most depressing of the messages I received. To me, truth, that is to say reality, is the only infallible guide. I would define Truth as God.

It is possible that a generation of black young men and women suffered because the terrorism and abuse they were enduring at home and were hoping to be liberated from, in literature and imagination, if not in life, was, among their elders, being debated as if it did not exist. How can the young trust us, if we lie about what they already know?

What will be the impact on coming generations if they are denied knowledge of evolution? If they are encouraged to ignore global warming? If no one teaches them where the "goodies" of the West come from? If leaders gloss over the widening enslavement of people in poor countries whose women and especially whose children are locked into foul, airless rooms for hours on end and forced to make cheap rugs and towels and clothing for a European and American market; women, children, and men "earning" as little as seven cents a day? This is modern-day slavery, and we should call it what it is.

Censoring what frightens or hurts us is understandable. In these times of so much bad news it is an attempt to protect the fragile self. But we may find ourselves cut off from friends and possible allies in this way; an undesirable side effect.

I overcame some of the pain of being driven from the community (which is what it often felt like) by sitting with the point of view of the people who attacked me; until I could plainly see their fear, and the reason for it. It was not helpful to attack me, but I could comprehend why they did so. Years of insecurity as creators, and as Americans, fueled their anxieties, not to mention years of doubt about their sexual attractiveness and its alleged superiority. They could not trust that my confidence in their human grace was so complete that I could write any number of novels critical of hurtful behavior without diminishing my faith. There was fear at not being seen in the full spectrum of their humanity and fear that my "truth" about God, sexuality, and nature meant that their inherited teachings about these things was "wrong." When I fully accepted the reality of their suffering from this fear, I could begin to feel compassion, rather than disgust, irritation, anger or, more likely in my case, mystification.

Today Americans, who used to feel welcomed wherever we went, travel abroad with trepidation. We know we are not trusted or liked, that we are even hated, by millions of people around the globe. We must ask ourselves why this is so and do the work of discovering our historical behavior toward the other countries and peoples of the planet. As disturbing as this will be, it is a first step toward a peaceful existence. Not because we can make peace for our country, but because we can make peace with ourselves by changing any harmful behavior or attitude that contributed to our present predicament. Choose any country on the map that appears to hate America. Listen to what people are shouting at their rallies and read what their banners proclaim in the street. Sit with their anger until you can see America through their eyes. Try to meet someone from Afghanistan, Palestine or Iran, Iraq or North Korea, Cuba or Nicaragua. The Philippines. Talk with Native Hawaiians about the American takeover and subsequent colonization of their country. Visit North American reservations. Remember that you, yourself, are America. The U.S. Behave as if you are the entire country and carry yourself with humility and dignity.

Love is not concerned
With whom you pray
Or where you slept
The night you ran away
From home

Love is concerned
That the beating of your heart
The beating of your heart
Should harm
No one

12.

Sent by Earth:
A Message from the
Grandmother Spirit

Talk given to the Midwives Alliance of
North America, September 22, 2001

The great danger in the world today is that the very
feeling and conception of what is a human being
might well be lost.

—Richard Wright to Jean-Paul Sartre (circa 1940),
in *Richard Wright* by Constance Webb

This quote seemed the perfect segue into my novel
The Third Life of Grange Copeland (1970), which
explores the challenge of remaining human under
the horrific conditions of American apartheid in
the Southern United States during my parents' and
grandparents' time. They and their children faced
massively destructive psychological and physical
violence from landowners—their successful dis-

possession and/or extermination of the indigenous people completed—who used every conceivable weapon to keep the sharecropping/slave-labor system intact. A system in which a relatively small ruling class of white people had as much food, land, space and cheap energy (black people's labor) to run their enterprises as they wanted while most people of color—including blacks, yellows, reds and browns—and many poor white people had barely enough of anything to keep themselves alive.

"We own our own souls, don't we?" is that novel's ringing, central cry.

It is the ringing central cry of our time.

I have been advised that there are several different groups of people in the audience; not just members of the Midwives Alliance of North America. I have been warned that some of these people are afraid I am going to talk only about birthin' and babies. However, I came to Albuquerque especially because I wish to be with midwives, whose business of birthin' and babies is, I believe, the most honorable on Earth.

A few days ago I was in the presence of Sobonfu Somé, a contemporary carrier of traditional, pre-colonial and perhaps pre-patriarchal, ancient African lifeways. She taught us that in her culture, among the Dagara people of Burkina Faso, the most important thing that happens in a person's life is that they be welcomed when they are born. If they are not welcomed, all their lives they experience a feeling of not quite having arrived. There is anxiety. There is unease. There is fear. This made me think of the title I had originally chosen for this talk, which changed after the bombing of the World Trade Center and the Pentagon, "Seeing the Light: The Importance of Being Properly Born." Some of you who attended my talk last year may recall my story of my own birth: the midwife and my grandmother were present in the room, but alas, they were busy chatting by the fireplace as my mother, overwhelmed with pain, fainted as I was being born. Several minutes passed before they knew what had happened. Was the fire going out? Were they busy, perhaps, restoring it? I realize that even at this late date I wish they'd been beside or, better, on the bed, waiting to receive me, instead of halfway across the room. And that my mother had been conscious.

I wished that even more after I witnessed a birth and saw a newborn being welcomed into its mother's arms, into the light of its father's smile, into the world and into its own community.

Sobonfu Somé then asked us to stand as I am now asking you to do, and to turn to the person on either side, take their hands, look them in the eye, and tell them: *I welcome you here.* Take your time doing this, there is no hurry. If this is a person you've never seen before, so much the better.

I'd like to read an address that I gave at a Peace

for Cuba rally on February 1st, 1992. The title is "The Story of Why I Am Here, or, A Woman Connects Oppressions; Putting My Arms Around Sadie Hussein, Age Three."

Last January (ten years ago) when the war against Iraq began, I was in Mexico writing a novel about a woman who is genitally mutilated in a ritual of female circumcision that her society imposes on all females. Genital mutilation (aka genital cutting) is a mental and physical health hazard that directly affects some one hundred million women and girls worldwide, alive today, to whom it has been done. Because of increased risk of trauma during delivery, it affects the children to whom they give birth. Indirectly, because of its linkage to the spread of AIDS, especially among women and children, it affects the health and well-being of everyone on the planet.

With no television or radio, and a lack of eagerness to see or hear arrogant Western males discussing their military prowess, their delight in their own "clean-handed" destructiveness, I relied on a friend's phone calls to his son in San Francisco to keep me informed. His son told us about the huge resistance in San Francisco to the war, which made me love the city even more than I did already, and informed us too that he had been one of those so outraged they'd closed down the Bay Bridge.

What to do? Go home and join the demonstrations, or continue to write about the fact that little girls' bodies are daily "bombed" by dull knives, rusty tin can tops and scissors, shards of unwashed glass—and that this is done to them not by a foreign power but by their own parents? I decided to stay put. To continue this story— which became *Possessing the Secret of Joy*— about female genital mutilation, which I believe is vital for the world to hear. But of course I could not forget the war being waged against the Earth and the people of Iraq.

Because I was thinking so hard about the suffering of little girls, while grieving over the frightened people trying to flee our government's bombs, my unconscious, in trying to help me balance my thoughts, did a quite wonderful thing. It gave me a substitute for Saddam Hussein, the solitary "demon" among tens of millions on whom the United States' military bombs were falling. Her name was Sadie Hussein, and she was three years old. So, as the bombs fell, I thought about Sadie Hussein, with her bright dark eyes and chubby cheeks, her shiny black curls and her dainty pink dress, and I put my arms around her. I could not, however, save her.

As it turned out, this was the truth. Saddam Hussein still reigns, at least as secure in his power over the Iraqis, according to some media sources, as George Bush is over North Americans. It is

Sadie Hussein who is being destroyed, and who, along with nine hundred thousand more Iraqi children under the age of five, is dying of cholera, malnutrition, infection and diarrhea. Since the war, fifty thousand such children have died. It is Sadie Hussein who starves daily on less than half her body's nutritional needs, while Saddam Hussein actually appears to have gained weight.

This is the story of why I am here today. I am here because I pay taxes. More money in taxes in one year than my sharecropping parents, descendents of enslaved Africans and Indians, earned in a lifetime. My taxes helped pay for Sadie Hussein's suffering and death. The grief I feel about this will accompany me to my grave. I believe war is a weapon of persons without personal power, that is to say, the power to reason, the power to persuade, from a position of morality and integrity; and that to go to war with any enemy who is weaker than you is to admit you possess no resources within yourself to bring to bear on your own fate. I will think of George Bush (senior) vomiting once into the lap of the Japanese prime minister—and every media considered this major news—and will immediately see hundreds of thousands of Iraqi children, cold, hungry, dying of fever, dysentery, typhoid, and every other sickness, vomiting endlessly into the laps of their mothers—who are also emaciated, starving, terrorized, and so illiterate they are unable to read Saddam Hussein's name, no matter how large he writes it.

Probably not a person in this room would bomb a baby, child or pregnant woman. Or cause elderly grandparents to starve or not have drinking water. *Probably not.* And yet, that is the position in which we find ourselves. The war against Iraq continues. In the ten years since I wrote my lament, millions more have died, the majority of them small children. Unlike most North Americans, I did not watch the initial bombing on television; I did later see, however, footage showing the bombing of a long line of what looked like old men trying to flee. They were running this way and that, their eyes filled with terror. I recognized more than I ever had that it is the very soul of the people of North America that is being lost, and that if this happens, for the rest of our time on the planet we are doomed to run with the dogs of war. *The dogs of war.* This is the vision that I have of this period. Ravenous, rapacious dogs, mad with greed and lust, red tongues out and salivating, running loose across the planet. They are the dogs that show up in some of the art of our time, in cartoons, or in the movie *Natural Born Killers.* It is an ancient image, however, and what astonishes me is how accurately and irresistibly it has arisen in the psyche. And the psyche recognizes this image, not because it is only external. But because some part of it is in-

ternal as well. Which means we must all look inside and get to know our own dogs of war. Some of
our war dogs, we have to own, are paying taxes
that will be used to destroy people almost identical
to us. Many of our war dogs are connected to heating our homes and fueling our cars.

A Native Person Looks Up from the Plate
Or, owning how we must look to a person
who has become our food.

They are eating
Us.
To step out of our doors
Is to feel
Their teeth
At our throats.

They are gobbling up our lands
Our waters
Our weaving
&
Our artifacts.

They are nibbling
At the noses
Of
Our canoes
& moccasins.

They drink our oil
Like cocktails
& lick down
Our jewelry
Like icicles.

They are
Siphoning
Our songs.

They are devouring
Us.
We brown, black
Red and yellow,
Unruly white
Morsels
Creating Life
Until we die.
Spread out in the chilling sun
That is
Their plate.

They are eating
Us raw
Without sauce.

Everywhere we
Have been
We are no more.
Everywhere we are

Going
They do not want.

They are eating
Us whole.
The glint of their
Teeth
The light
That beckons
Us to table
Where only they
Will dine.

They are devouring
Us.
Our histories.
Our heroes.
Our ancestors.
And all appetizing
Youngsters
To come.

Where they graze
Among
The people
Who create
Who labor
Who live
In beauty
And walk

So lightly
On the earth
There is nothing
Left.

Not even our roots
Reminding us
To bloom.

Now they have wedged
The whole
Of the earth
Between their
Cheeks.

Their
Wide bellies
Crazily clad
In stolen goods
Are near
To bursting
With
The fine meal
Gone foul
That is us.

Where do we start? How do we reclaim a proper relationship to the world?

Here's an old story the world has recently found and loves:

In the Babemba tribe of South Africa, when a person acts irresponsibly or unjustly, he is placed in the center of the village, alone and unfettered.

All work ceases, and every man, woman and child in the village gathers in a large circle around the accused individual. Then each person in the tribe speaks to the accused, one at a time, about all the good things the person in the center of the circle has done in his lifetime. Every incident, every experience that can be recalled with any detail and accuracy is recounted. All his positive attributes, good deeds, strengths and kindnesses are recited carefully and at length.

The tribal ceremony often lasts several days. At the end, the tribal circle is broken, a joyous celebration takes place, and the person is symbolically and literally welcomed back into the tribe.

This will not be the fate of Osama bin Laden, accused of masterminding the attack on North America. In a war on Afghanistan, he will either be left alive, while thousands of impoverished, frightened people, most of them women and children and the elderly, are bombed into oblivion around him, or he will be killed in a bombing attack for which he seems, in his spirit—from what I have gleaned from news sources—quite prepared. In his mind, he is fighting a holy war against the United States. To die in battle against it would be an honor. He has been quoted as saying he would like to make the United States into a "shadow of itself" as he helped make the Soviet Union, which lost the war in Afghanistan, become a shadow of itself. In fact, he appears to take credit for helping the Soviet Union disintegrate. I personally would like him to understand that the shadow he wishes upon us, of poverty, fear, an almost constant state of terror, is merely the America too many of us already know. It is certainly the shadow my ancestors lived with for several hundred years.

But what would happen to his cool armor if he could be reminded of all the good, nonviolent things he has done? Further, what would happen to him if he could be brought to understand the preciousness of the lives he has destroyed? I firmly believe the only punishment that works is love. Or, as the Buddha said: Hatred will never cease by hatred. By love alone is it healed.

Recommendation

Promise me
Promise me this day,
Promise me now,
While the sun is overhead
Exactly at the zenith,
Promise me.

Even as they
Strike you down

With the mountain of hatred and violence;
Even as they step on you and crush you
Like a worm,
Even as they dismember and disembowel you,
Remember, brother,
Remember:
Man is not your enemy.

The only thing worthy of you is compassion—
Invincible, limitless, unconditional.
Hatred will never let you face
The beast in man.

One day, when you face this beast alone,
With your courage intact, your eyes kind,
Untroubled
(even as no one sees them)
Out of your smile
Will bloom a flower.
And those who love you
Will behold you
Across ten thousand worlds of birth and dying.
　　　　　—from *Call Me By My True Names*
　　　　　by Thich Nhat Hanh

Thich Nhat Hanh, beloved Buddhist monk and peace practitioner, wrote this poem in 1965 for the young people he worked with who risked their lives every day during the war in Vietnam. Remember that war? The napalmed naked children fleeing down a flaming road? He wrote it to recommend that they prepare to die without hatred. Some of them had already been killed violently, and he cautioned the others against hating. He told them:

> Our enemy is our anger, hatred, greed, fanaticism, and discrimination against (each other). If you die because of violence, you must meditate on compassion in order to forgive those who kill you. When you die realizing this state of compassion, you are truly a child of The Awakened One. Even if you are dying in oppression, shame, and violence, if you can smile with forgiveness, you have great power.

Thich Nhat Hanh reminds us that "Where there is a mature relationship between people, there is always compassion and forgiveness." This observation is crucial to how we must now, more than ever, understand our world. Every thought, every act, every gesture must be in the direction of developing and maintaining a mature relationship with the peoples of the planet; all thought of domination, control, force and violence must be abandoned.

S M

I tell you, Chickadee
I am afraid of people

Who cannot cry
Tears left unshed
Turn to poison
In the ducts
Ask the next soldier you see
Enjoying a massacre
If this is not so.

People who do not cry
Are victims
Of soul mutilation
Paid for in Marlboros
And trucks.

Violence does not work
Except for the man
Who pays your salary
Who knows
If you could still weep
You would not take the job.
     —from *Horses Make a Landscape Look More*
      Beautiful by Alice Walker

As Clarissa Pinkola Estés, master *contadora* and *curandera*, points out, while it is true that the soul can never be destroyed, it can certainly leave us and take up residence elsewhere. I was struck by how many people I talked to after the bombing of the World Trade Towers and the Pentagon said they were numb. Felt nothing. Or didn't know what to feel. I myself experienced a sensation of hollowness. Emptiness. Insubstantiality. I felt weak, slightly nauseous, as if part of my own body were disintegrating. I knew enough to let myself experience all my feelings, whatever they were. At one point I remember laughing because one of our leaders, perhaps at a loss for something to say and to put a quick us-versus-them spin on the deeply traumatic events, called the pilots of the planes that had gone into the Trade Towers "cowards." It was not a word that came to my mind at all. In fact, when I watched the suicide glide of the plane into the second tower, what I saw, and instantly recognized, was pain. And desperation. Disconnection. Alienation. And a closed-hearted, despairing courage, too, to sacrifice one's life (along with the lives of thousands of others) to make a point. What is the story whose fiery end I am witnessing? I wondered. This was an act by a man who did not believe in the possibility of love, or even common sense, to transform the world. I can easily imagine there will be thousands like him born in our time, that from the roots of this one man's story, they will come to birth practically every minute; and our government will not be remotely able to "smoke" all of them "out of their holes." The world being what it is, some of those "holes" are likely to be uncomfortably close to us.

What are we going to feel like, if we kill thousands of people who somewhat resemble this man?

I can tell you; we are not going to feel fine. We are not going to feel happy. Some of us, perhaps the very young, will feel triumphant and larger than life for three weeks or so. After that, we will begin to wonder who exactly it was that we killed. And why. And whether a hungry, naked boy herding goats on a land mine–saturated hill was the right guy.

Murder, after all, is murder. Even if it is done in war. It is very intimate. The beings we kill become, somehow, ours for life. Ironically, we become responsible for them in death as we were not in life. With time, we are going to be reminded of a few facts that speak to this: that, for instance, during the Vietnam War, in which America bombed a country most Americans up to then had never heard of, fifty thousand Americans died. But since the end of the war, more than sixty thousand who were in the war have died from suicide and drug overdoses and other ailments of the spirit and soul. George Bush *père* counseled us to "put the war [that war] behind us." But as Michael Meade, magical storyteller and warrior/mythologist, so emphatically reminds us, when speaking of that war, in which he refused to fight: "What is behind us is a long, long row of coffins and we'd better turn around and genuinely grieve and give our dead, both Vietnamese and American, a proper burial. Then we might be able to talk about going on." It is not too hard to imagine that those who are now calling for war, so many of them old men, have not engaged their true feelings in so long that they think to bomb country after country is to grieve.

What grieving is not:

Grieving is not the same as massacre.

Grieving is not the same as shopping.

Grieving is not the same as overeating.

Grieving is not the same as worrying about one's weight. (Or color, sex or age).

Grieving is not the same as trying to stay young.

Grieving is not the same as coloring your hair a new shade each month to forget you've given money that will be used to blow off people's heads.

Grieving is not the same as seeing the shadow in everyone but yourself.

To grieve is above all to acknowledge loss, to understand that there is a natural end to endless gain.

To grieve means to come to an understanding, finally, of inevitable balance; life will right itself, though how it does this remains, and will doubtless remain, mysterious.

The Taliban in Afghanistan, for instance, who have treated the indigenous women with such brutal contempt that thousands have been driven to suicide, now face at least a moment in time when theirs is the position of the women they have tortured. It will always be so.

It is this natural balancing of life that we fear; that is why, given the history of our own country, many feel a need to be protected by Star Wars defense systems.

At this time of mourning
May we be connected to each other,
May we know the range and depth of feelings in
ourselves and in
Each other
There is vulnerability, fear, love, rage, hatred,
compassion,
Courage, despair, and
Hope in ourselves, each other, and the world.
May we know our most authentic feelings
And voice them when we speak.
May we tap into soul and spirit when we are silent
together.
May healing begin in us.
May we form and become a circle.

Begin by holding hands in a circle (even two people
can be a circle)
Be silent and feel the clasp and connection
Of hands and heart.
Then each in turn
Speak for yourself
And listen to each other.
   Put judgment aside
   Remember that anything voiced that you want

to silence
May be a silenced part of yourself.
Sing what spontaneously wants to be sung.
And end each circle as it was begun.
Hold hands once again, hold silence (for
meditation, contemplation, prayer),
Invite blessings,
Until we meet again.

I received this R_x from Jean Shinoda Bolen, M.D., master healer of the psyche and author of *The Millionth Circle* among many other books. She writes:

A circle is a healing and connecting prescription accessible to everyone. Every family, any group of people anywhere can form one. In preparation for the 5th UN Conference on Women and the United General Assembly Special Session on Children, the Millionth Circle 2005 planning committee wrote this statement of intention: "Circles encourage connection and cooperation among their members and inspire compassionate solutions to individual, community and world problems. We believe that circles support each member to find her or his own voice and to live more courageously. Therefore, we intend to see and nurture circles, wherever possible, in order to cultivate equality, sustainable livelihoods, preservation of the earth and peace for all. Our aim is to celebrate the millionth circle as the metaphor of an idea whose time has come."

The metaphor "the millionth circle" was taken from the title of Jean's book, which in turn was inspired by "the story of the 'hundredth monkey' and morphic field theory that sustained activists in the 1970–'80s in the face of conventional wisdom that said ordinary people could not deter the nuclear arms race."

Jean advises:

Wherever you are today, tomorrow, next week— bring people (include the children) together to form circles. If you are in a group, transform it into a circle, if you are already in a circle, get together. In response to the destruction of buildings, families, lives and everyone's sense of security, this is something you can do to help.

I have been part of a circle for many years. It is one of the most important connections of my life. One reason the circle is so powerful is that it is informed, in fact shaped by, the Grandmother Spirit. The spirit of impartiality, equality, equanimity. Of nurturing but also of fierceness. It has no use for hierarchy. Or patriarchy. Tolerates violence against itself for a while, but will sooner or later rise to defend itself. This is the spirit of the Earth itself.

And so, today, I feel sent to you, midwives of North America, by the Earth Herself. You are, against the cruelest odds of history and laws, attempting to bring human beings into the world in a way that welcomes them. I have seen your work and know it is essential in getting humankind back on the right track. Women must be supported, loved, listened to, cared for, as we are carrying life and attempting to deliver it to our world. To us, Life's community, not to the war machine. The child must be able to feel, emerging from the womb, that we are honored it is here. We are thrilled. We are called upon in this frightful time to labor for the body and the soul.

We must learn nothing less than how to be born again.

Just as the body loves exercise, though it complains, the soul loves awareness. For a long time I've pondered the expression "Never let the right hand know what the left hand is doing." This advice, I believe, is wrong. We must struggle to see both our hands, and their activity, clearly. We must see, for instance, the Palestinians and what has happened to their homes, their fields, and their trees; and we must see what is happening to the Israelis and their homes and their fields and their trees. We must see where our tax dollars flow and try, in awareness, to follow them. We, as Americans, have a hand in each nation's fate, but we tend to look only at the hand the news media shows us, constantly. The situation in the Middle East, a war between brothers and cousins, may mean the end of life as we in North America know it. It may ultimately mean our lives. The soul wants to know the truth; what is really going on. Nor must we fall asleep while Afghanistan, a country with seven hundred thousand disabled orphans, is being bombed. We must struggle to stay awake enough to imagine what it feels like to be small and afraid, not to have parents, to be disabled, to be hungry and lonely, and not be able, either, to get out of the way of America's wrath. The soul wants to know why we have paid taxes to support the Taliban. Why, through that group, we have so heartlessly supported the debasement and assassination of the Feminine.

While we trudge onward, trying to remember what Black Elk observed: that all living beings are essentially alike, I recommend the wearing of two threads of different colors, one of them, representing the Feminine, red. The red thread should be worn on the left wrist, closest to the heart, and the brown or white or black thread, representing whatever endangers the Feminine, the Grandmother, Earth, on the right. These will remind us to stay awake.

It will also help, I think, to create an altar, especially for our children who make up so much of the military. It should be kept beautiful with flowers and candles and bowed to every day. There is no way most of them will ever understand who they are killing or why. The souls of many of them will go so far from their bodies during war that they will never return. There should be feathers and stones and other meaningful objects on this altar, but above all, there should be a mirror. And pictures of our loved ones who never knew what struck them on the 11th of September. Together they, our children, and the children our children will kill, will create a circle; let us acknowledge that.

While thinking of the Grandmother Spirit that I believe should be guiding Earth, and must, for humans to survive, I thought of three women, all unmarried as far as I know, two of them childless, all relatively young. Still, they exemplify the spirit of which I speak. They are Julia Butterfly Hill, who sat in a redwood tree for two years trying to save it from being cut down; thus bringing attention to the massive assault on our forests; Amy Goodman, of *Democracy Now!,* who has clung to the airwaves to bring us truly informative radio; and Representative Barbara Lee, who alone voted not to give away the Congress's (and therefore the people's) right to declare war. I invoke their names to honor them in this gathering of wise, strong women who will understand exactly how this kind of courage differs from the kind that speaks calmly of "collateral damage," i.e. obliteration of infants, pregnant women and small children, old men running in terror meted out from the sky.

On the day of the bombings I realized why Christians cross themselves. And why the people of Islam turn toward Mecca. I knew that I also need a gesture of self-blessing that would, at the same time, symbolize blessing and protection of the world and its varied inhabitants.

I realized we, as humans, need a New World peace *mudra* and chant to help us through the days ahead, which will undoubtedly cause unprecedented suffering and pain. Partly because more people than ever before will be conscious of what is transpiring. And untold thousands will feel completely helpless to do anything about it.

Spirit, the Grandmother Spirit of Earth, sent me this mudra and chant:

The mudra is to hold the thumb and first two fingers together, symbolizing unity, while making a circle around one's heart. And as much of the body as one feels like covering. This is done three times while chanting:

One Earth
One People
One Love

One Earth
One People
One Love

One Earth
One People
One Love

Please stand and let us together chant this blessing seven times; seven is the ideal number of people in a circle that is designed to grow the soul and change the world.

13.

Orchids

A talk at the Yoga Summit & Retreat
Presented by International Association of
Black Yoga Teachers
Watsonville, California
August 1, 2003

At some point in my life, perhaps beginning in my forties, I began to notice that, in addition to cut-flower bouquets, people were beginning to give me orchids. I have always lived amid an abundance of flowers, but never orchids. They seemed exotic and a bit strange. I admired their beauty, watered them whenever I thought of it. Sometimes sat them close to the bathtub to let them enjoy moisture while I bathed. Beyond that I did not know how to care for them. They seemed mysterious. Fragile. Foreign. Sure enough, once they'd bloomed and I watered them once or twice hoping to induce more blooms, they no longer held my interest. Slowly their wide, fat green leaves turned brown, spiders began to inhabit the tree bark they nestled in, and, within a few weeks, these spectacular plants that had so enchanted me, still alive, but barely, were on their way out the door.

How did this change?

One day, after receiving several orchids at once, all lovely beyond belief and appearing to me at the time as the most miraculous of flowers—after all, they were not even planted in dirt—I resolved to do better by them, in honor of their beauty. I had also, on my travels about the world, notably in Hawaii and Mexico, noticed that orchids, which I had considered so fragile and unique, grew casually, elegantly, profusely, in rotten logs and ordinary trees. Surely I could keep a couple of them going in my house.

The florist from whom many of my orchid gifts had come repotted the ones I sent to her and offered instructions: immerse the plants in water once a week or so; mist blooms and leaves each morning; place where the plants can enjoy reflected sunlight.

I followed these simple instructions and now have a rustic antique Thai chair (my plant stand) filled to overflowing with healthy, blooming orchids.

Can it be this simple?

The other day an old acquaintance and I were talking about weighty matters in his life. As an afterthought, and after detailing his recent religious conversion following years of both using and selling cocaine—some of which he sold to children in his own family—his voice brightened. Listen up, he said. Guess what? At the Kingdom Hall (where he now goes in search of acceptance and salvation) there is a little girl, chubby, black, with the roundest cheeks (earlier in his life he had been repelled by chubbiness, blackness and femaleness) and she's so smart. But nobody in her family even knows what she's talking about most of the time. They all watch television; she reads. You know they did a study that proves the more television you watch, the less you understand anything. It's like she and her family are talking about two different worlds.

But, he continued, I still read, and have always read, so she and I can talk to each other. And the other day, her father thanked me for taking the time to talk to her about what she's reading. He says the difference in her is profound. That she's not so angry anymore. And guess what else? One day she said: You give me so much and I don't have anything to give you back. And I said: How about a kiss. And when I bent down close to her, she kissed me on the forehead! He chortled with joy, while I listened, amazed. He had not sounded this happy when he bought his first drug-sponsored Cadillac.

Is it this easy?

You have invited me to your yoga retreat to talk, presumably, at least a little, about yoga, which I practice intermittently. Several of my teachers are in the audience. However, as I thought about this talk, the enthusiasm I felt for giving it came from the idea that under the guise of talking about yoga I could talk about something that I've contemplated for decades: what is it that makes us black? What, in fact, does it mean to be black?

While I was pondering this question, I was also living in North America, in the United States, where having black skin was a crime during all the years black people were locked up in slavery. Now of course the crime that can keep you locked up forever is possession of a drug, or violent behavior, or being arrested three times for possession or violence. You become part of a prison plantation system and I would imagine that for the hundreds of thousands of incarcerated black people it is as if time has stopped: somewhere in the fifteenth to the nineteenth centuries.

Whenever I think of what blackness is, I think of night. There it is, following each and every day, faithful as the sun. Everything gestates and grows then, in the restful dark. I think of black hollyhocks with their magical hint of red; I think of those black polished stones the Japanese obviously revere because they use them in so many places. I think of black skin. When I am in Senegal, where some of the blackest people live, I am awestruck by the beauty of their skin. It is like night, and like black hollyhocks (in their case, there is a hint of blue); it is like polished black stones that feel charged with energy, over which their sweat, like water in a river, runs, causing a glistening that, moon-like, reflects light. When I am in Senegal, where some of the blackest and most attractive people live, I am in pain a lot of the time because the business in skin bleaching creams is so strong. There are women whose faces are raw and red from bleaching and because they can not afford to cover more than their faces it is as if they are wearing masks. Which of course they are.

What does it mean to self-eradicate?

I engage this question every time I play with my hair, which is turning gray. I like the gray, and yet, there are times when I feel bored by it. As I experiment with various colorations, wanting to honor my gray and yet wanting also to honor my passion for variety and change, I feel concern for my own integrity. Some of my friends laugh at me: it doesn't matter at all what you do with your hair, they say. Wear it blond, wear it red. Who cares? But we are a people who have had to suffer for the right to wear our hair as it grows, a prerequisite to loving it, and ourselves, as we are; the struggle for hair liberation does not, I feel, stop at nappiness. What about salt and pepper? What about gray? What about white? And yet, my friends are right to honor the freedom of spirit implicit in choosing red or blond hair. If indeed it is freedom of spirit and not the sad response of the briefly free to the siren call of modern colonial advertising. If it is a freedom of choice uncontaminated by fear.

A Chinese American friend streaks his dark hair with red every year in honor of Chinese New Year. He laughed when I asked whether it had anything to do with being dark-haired in Anglo-imaged America. And perhaps this is the freedom to which we might aspire. The freedom that comes with self-acceptance, and goes beyond, to the point Mozart reached when, on being offered three outrageous bouffant wigs from which to choose (in the wonderful movie *Amadeus*) he chose all three; because they were all, he said, so lovely. One of them was flamingo pink.

So what does this have to do with being black? Everything. It is black to struggle with issues like this. It is black to care.

And the reason it is black to care has to do with memory and with revelation. Which is the time we are living in now. Everything you have ever wondered about or wanted to know is being remembered or revealed, during this period. Partly this is because of telecommunications and our ability to be aware of remote places and activities around the globe, but it is more the result of the presence in the world of so many awakened women.

Sometimes, when I am asked to give a talk, I simply set aside the three or four issues that rise to the top of my pile as I'm working at my desk. For this talk there are three issues that somehow want to be worked into this meditation about yoga.

As some of you know, for about a decade I was deeply involved in the effort to illuminate the danger to the health of women and their societies posed by female genital mutilation. I met and was inspired, early on, by a woman who had dedicated her life to this work, Hanny Lightfoot Klein. She and her immediate family escaped Nazi Germany to settle in the United States. The rest of her kin, as she says, "went up the chimney." It is partly her Jewishness, and certainly her feeling of indebtedness to Jewish culture, as well as what she calls her "survivor guilt," that has made her a staunch ally to the mutilated women she encountered in, primarily, African countries. In a letter that she wrote to me a few weeks ago she writes:

> There does seem to be a noticeable remission going on where FGM is concerned—in patches here and there so far, but one where it is possible to trust its veracity. Women have begun to assert themselves, to take their lives into their own hands and to reject the role of "victim," such as they had always accepted as immutable before now. It is a beautiful thing to see happening at last. What a joy!

I was reminded of a very tense moment I experienced on the Michael Jackson show (no relation to Michael Jackson the singer) in Los Angeles as I toured the country speaking about female genital mutilation and male circumcision, which I considered also very harmful. I thought it possible, and said so on this show, that the circumcision of boy babies enhanced their later acceptance of violence and of war. An irate Jewish man called the station and for several minutes screamed at me. He was outraged that I dared speak on behalf of the Jewish child who must undergo circumcision as a matter of identity as a Jew.

In an interview Lightfoot Klein also sent me, "Circumcised Babies Are More Nervous," there is a succinct explanation of some of my other concerns.

The interviewer asks: How do you explain these worldwide predilections for barbarities against the genitals?

To which Lightfoot Klein answers:

I was told about one African ethnic group whose initiation rites involved the removal of one testicle. Holocaust survivors from one of the concentration camps relate something quite similar. This particular Nazi doctor cut off one of the Jews' testicles, and warned: "Just wait. Next time I get the second one." Foreskin circumcision of infants is in essence a low-grade castration. The nervous system perceives it as such. Total obedience is achieved with the threat of complete castration, and most especially when this threat occurs at an age when the child is not yet able to understand

and only feels. This makes the fear even greater. It pervades the individual's entire life.

Until I traveled to Africa and later researched female genital mutilation, which is done to children forbidden even to scream, I had not understood how black people had been and still are enslaved by a tradition in Africa, just as perhaps Jews, especially the men, were enslaved before they arrived there, in Egypt.

In any event, it is black to care about the suffering of children, whatever color or tribe. The Feminine, considered black or "dark," whether in men or women, hears the cries of others, and it is the Feminine that, until recently, we have honored in ourselves. Now many of us wish to be the men that white men are. But that will in no way deliver us and the world from suffering.

Memory and Revelation: Revelation and Memory

A few months ago I visited Japan on a book tour. My publisher there, Shueisha, had published six of my books and was poised to publish a seventh before I felt any interest in visiting Japan. I had a vague idea why my books were popular there—the Japanese woman is struggling against an entrenched, cruel and insidious patriarchal system that has robbed her from time immemorial of her freedom and identity. This makes her awakening in our time similar to that happening to women across the globe. I knew about the viciousness of Japanese soldiers during World War II, and the abuse of mostly Korean "comfort women" during that war, and the refusal of the Japanese courts to pay reparations to the elderly survivors. I knew, from reading history books, of the Japanese domination of China, before the Chinese drove them out. And I knew a bit about Japanese poetry and cars, of which I've read much and owned several. Nothing, however, had prepared me for the sweetness, graciousness and kindness of the Japanese people, including the men, that I encountered. After nine days of working with the people who translate, publish and promote my books, I felt part of a team, cared for as if I were family. On the second or third day after I arrived, word went out that I had caught a cold. Every single person we worked with and even met in interviews brought me his or her favorite medicine. And prepared it for me, if I didn't know how; which I didn't since I don't speak or read Japanese. As I joked with them at the Tokyo Book Fair: I was brought so much medicine, the medicine almost made me sick! This experience of being cared for by a company I was working with has never happened to me in almost forty years of publishing in the USA. This caring about me as well as about the number of books my presence in Japan might sell seemed very black to me.

And yet, there was a recent article in the *San*

Francisco Chronicle, "A Bad Week for Women in Japan," that exposed a side of the Japanese leadership that, like information about their behavior during war, or their abuse and disdain of the "comfort women" male soldiers had abused and discarded, made me very sad.

> The dispute [over whether working women should receive pensions as working men do] erupted after a panel discussion last week in which former Prime Minister Yoshiro Mori and other senior political leaders debated how Japan should address its declining birth rate.
>
> Mori, [present Prime Minister] Koizumi's mentor and predecessor, said women who do not have children should not be allowed to claim pensions.
>
> "Welfare is supposed to take care of and reward those women who have lots of children," Mori said. "It is truly strange to say we have to use tax money to take care of women who don't even give birth once, who grow old living their lives selfishly and singing the praises of freedom."
>
> During the debate, ruling Liberal Democratic Party lawmaker and former cabinet minister Seiichi Ota said a growing number of Japanese men seem to lack the courage to propose marriage.
>
> The debate's moderator then referred to a recent high-profile case of gang rape allegedly involving students at several prestigious universities.

"At least gang rapists are still vigorous," Ota replied. "Isn't that at least a little closer to normal?"

At a later point, after several Japanese women complained, another high-ranking official claimed gang rapes were the fault of women. "The problem is that there are lots of women dressed provocatively," he said.

I believe men, no less than women, wish to be perceived as beautiful. Men can be beautiful and many men are. I met beautiful men in Japan. But it is important that men realize they can not be beautiful sounding like this. It is as if vipers and scorpions and toads are dropping from their lips.

Where is the blackness of caring that I had so appreciated in the Japanese? Not evident in these leaders of the people, who obviously don't consider the female half of their population autonomous humans. It is painful to think that every one of these men, so lacking in empathy for their sisters, was raised by a Japanese woman, and that it is the labor of the Japanese woman, beginning with the labor to bring the Japanese man into the world, on which the entire society rests. These men sat around worried about the decline of the Japanese birthrate while exhibiting to everyone but themselves why a Japanese woman would have to be insane to want any more men like them born.

In the Sixties, that glorious decade of black

awakening, everyone had an idea about what blackness was. Dr. King said it was beautiful, a radical notion. For many people black was anger. *Anger.* It was such a liberation to let that part of our blackness show. It had been suppressed for hundreds of years. We were so happy to have it back, we became enamored of it; gazed at it with love. Until, like all things that are loved, it grew. Soon our anger crowded out every other aspect of blackness. Our gentleness went into hiding, our respectful behavior, our veneration of our teachers and our elders, our deep solidarity with the less-fortunate. Our loyalty to community. We began to accept leaders who tampered with the truth. When in fact, any of our elders could have told us, and unquestionably tried to: You cannot be led to a good place by anyone who lies, because obviously they have lost the way. I can only imagine the shock our elders have felt, watching the behavior of some of us; truth, in their world, was black.

In an article in *Amnesty NOW*, published by Amnesty International in the summer of 2003, titled "Soul Wound: The Legacy of Native American Schools," there is a harrowing account of how Native American children were treated in the white-run boarding schools especially set up in the 1800s to rid them of their Indian-ness.

At this point, while writing this talk and after reading this article for the second time, I had to get up from my desk, walk out into the countryside, sit on a bench—where my part-Cherokee mother had liked to sit before she died—and cry. Following this, I took out my yoga mat.

"Native Americans know all too well the reality of the boarding schools," writes Native American Bar Association President Richard Monette, who attended a North Dakota boarding school, "where recent generations learned the fine art of standing in line single-file for hours without moving a hair, as a lesson in discipline; where our best and brightest earned graduation certificates for homemaking and masonry; where the sharp rules of immaculate living were instilled through blistered hands and knees on the floor with scouring toothbrushes; where mouths were scrubbed with lye and chlorine solutions for uttering Native words.

"Sammy Toineeta (Lakota) helped found the national Boarding School Healing Project to document such abuses. 'Human rights activists must talk about the issue of boarding schools,' says Toineeta. 'It is one of the grossest human rights violations because it targeted children and was the tool for perpetrating cultural genocide. To ignore this issue would be to ignore the human rights of indigenous peoples, not only in the U.S., but around the world.' "

The schools were part of Euro-America's drive to solve the "Indian problem" and end Native control of their lands. While some colonizers advocated outright physical extermination, Captain Richard H. Pratt thought it wiser to "kill the Indian and save the man." In 1897 Pratt, an army veteran of the Indian wars, opened the first federally sanctioned boarding school: the Carlisle Industrial Training School in Carlisle, Penn.

"Transfer the savage-born infant to the surroundings of civilization, and he will grow to possess a civilized language and habit," said Pratt. He modeled Carlisle on a prison school he had developed for a group of 72 Indian prisoners of war at Florida's Fort Marion prison. His philosophy was to "elevate" American Indians to white standards through a process of forced acculturation that stripped them of their language, culture, and customs.

In an article packed with information about the destructiveness of this effort, there is the following:

Native scholars describe the destruction of their culture as a "soul wound" from which Native Americans have not healed. Embedded deep within that wound is a pattern of sexual and physical abuse that began in the early years of the boarding school system. Joseph Gone describes a history of "unmonitored and unchecked physical and sexual aggression perpetrated by school officials against a vulnerable and institutionalized population."

Rampant sexual abuse at reservation schools continued until the end of the 1980s. . . . In 1987 the FBI found evidence that John Boone, a teacher at the BIA-run Hopi day school in Arizona had sexually abused as many as 142 boys from 1979 until his arrest in 1987.

The abuse has dealt repeated blows to the traditional social structure of Indian communities. Before colonization, Native women generally enjoyed high status, according to scholars, and violence against women, children and elders was virtually nonexistent. Today, sexual abuse and violence have reached epidemic proportions in Native communities, along with alcoholism and suicide. By the end of the 1990s the sexual assault rate among Native Americans was three and a half times higher than for any other ethnic group in the U.S., according to the Department of Justice's Bureau of Justice statistics. Alcoholism in Native communities is currently six times higher than the national average. Researchers are just beginning to establish quantitative links between these epidemic rates and the legacy of boarding schools.

A more complete history of the abuses endured by Native American children exists in the accounts of survivors of Canadian "residential schools." Canada imported the U.S. boarding school model in the 1880s and maintained it well into the 1970s—four decades after the United States ended its stated policy of forced enrollment. Abuses in Canadian schools are better documented because survivors of Canadian schools are more numerous, younger, and generally more willing to talk about their experiences.

A 2001 report by the Truth Commission into Genocide in Canada documents the responsibility of the Roman Catholic Church, the United Church of Canada, the Anglican Church of Canada, and the federal government in the deaths of more than 50,000 Native children in the Canadian residential school system.

The report says church officials killed children by beating, poisoning, electric shock, starvation, prolonged exposure to sub-zero cold while naked, and medical experimentation, including the removal of organs and radiation exposure. In 1928 Alberta passed legislation allowing school officials to forcibly sterilize Native girls; British Columbia followed suit in 1933. There is no accurate toll of forced sterilizations because hospital staff destroyed records in 1995 after police launched an investigation. But according to the testimony of a nurse in Alberta, doctors sterilized entire groups of Native children when they reached puberty. The report also says that Canadian clergy, police, and business and government officials "rented out" children from the residential schools to pedophile rings.

The consequences of sexual abuse can be devastating. "Of the first 29 men who publicly disclosed sexual abuse in Canadian residential schools, 22 committed suicide," says Gerry Oleman, a counselor to residential school survivors in British Columbia.

Randy Fred (Tsehaht First Nation), a 47-year-old survivor, told the British Columbia Aboriginal Network on Disability Society, 'We were kids when we were raped and victimized. All the plaintiffs I've talked with have attempted suicide. I attempted suicide twice, when I was 19 and again when I was 20. We all suffered from alcohol abuse, drug abuse. Looking at the lists of students [abused in the school], at least half of the guys are dead."

The Truth Commission report says that the grounds of several schools contain unmarked graveyards of murdered schoolchildren, including babies born to Native girls raped by priests and other church officials in the school. Thousands of survivors and relatives have filed lawsuits against Canadian churches and governments since the 1990s, with the costs of settlements estimated at more than $1 billion. Many cases are still working their way through the court system.

Although there is disagreement in Native communities about how to approach the past, most agree that the first step is documentation. "It is crucial that this history be exposed," says

Willetta Dolphus, a Cheyenne River Lakota. "When the elders who were abused in these schools have the chance to heal, then the younger generation will begin to heal."

Members of the Boarding School Healing Project say that current levels of violence and dysfunction in Native communities result from human rights abuses perpetrated by state policy. In addition to setting up hotlines and healing services for survivors this broad coalition is using a human rights framework to demand accountability from Washington and churches.

While this project is Herculean in its scope, its success could be critical to the healing of indigenous nations from both contemporary and historical human rights abuses. Native communities, the project's founders hope, will begin to view the abuse as the consequence of human rights violations perpetrated by church and state rather than as individual failings. And for individuals, overcoming the silence and the stigma of abuse in Native communities can lead to breakthroughs: "There was an experience that caused me to be damaged," said boarding school survivor Sammy Toineeta. "I finally realized that there wasn't something wrong with me."

Many of us have Native American great-grandmothers. Though some of us were forced to deny her during our own black cultural revolution, that occurred, along with our enlightenment, during the Sixties and Seventies. Envious of, or offended by, straightness of hair or lighter color of skin or shape of nose, and wanting to pledge allegiance only to the African in us, we forbade mention of this ancestor, to whom we are so irrevocably linked, not through hair or skin or nose, but through suffering.

We know that everything I have listed here, everything that was done to Native American children, and to their parents (and to the Maori and the Hawaiians and the Tahitians and the Nunga of Australia, etc.), was done to our people. Mixed African and Indian and European, as we became. And more specific cruelties, numberless and un- speakable, that resulted from having sadists un- leashed upon them. Sadists wearing cassocks and rosaries, sadists pretending to be interested in God. Sadists who claimed to be bringing civiliza- tion. Sadists who inspired the more documented and endlessly spotlighted atrocities of Adolf Hitler. Sadists who clear-cut the spirits and souls of our ancestors as effectively as their slave-driving, white-supremacist greed clear-cut and devastated the land.

Lying on my yoga mat, having done a few back stretches taught me by Konda Mason, who sur- vives and thrives in our own time, I let go of all of this. I concentrate on my breath, and silently thank the Creator for allowing it to flow into and out of me. It is such a joy to know to do this.

I learned my first yoga postures while living in a tense and sadist-filled Mississippi, from a book for children called *Be a Fish, a Bird, a Tree!* It was years before I received instruction from an actual person. When I lived in San Francisco I took lessons once a week from the founder of Bikram yoga. And for many years after that practiced using a tape given to me by Quincy Jones, who, during our first meeting, demonstrated all the most difficult Hatha postures, effortlessly, including the fixed firm, which I was never able to do. Years later I encountered Konda Mason, a wonderful teacher of inspiring soul, and then Tajma Noor, a young master of yoga and a fabulous singer too, and then Deni Hodges, whose dedication and affection, while teaching me yoga, is blackness itself.

From the final *sevasana* of the yoga mat it is easy to see how like orchids we have been, and still are. Beautiful, rare, common, fragile, strong, exotic, plain. Gorgeous. And how true it is to say, as one can easily observe in many of our neighborhoods, where killing ourselves and each other has become almost a sport, we have no idea how to take care of us.

Until sadist rule of the world ends, or at least until it is revealed, acknowledged and controlled within human beings, we will never know peace. That is why yoga and meditation are essential. In order to free ourselves we must listen to many harrowing tales that our people, for their own health and sanity, must share with us. Knowing what happened to our ancestors' lives is the only way we can begin deconstruction of the dysfunction in our own. To do this will require the warriorship we associate generally with heroic leaders: Mandela, Che, King, Tubman, Truth, Malcolm X, etc. But it is within reach of us all. Warriorship in this case means holding protective *chi*, or life force, that enables one's self and the community to heal.

Which brings me to the question I posed at the beginning of my talk: What is blackness? What is it that makes us black?

To be black means to have body and soul together. That is why, customarily, we used to define a "together" person as "having soul." It has been shocking, in the past decades, to see so many soulless black people. People who, in our grandparents' time, would have been considered zombies. And it is this area in which yoga can be so powerful. Yoga means to bind back, unite. To bring the body and the soul together. To strengthen ensoulment. For this reason the practice of yoga is a holy endeavor and the teaching of it to our people a very high calling.

A marvelous thing happens when the body and soul are together, something that is the essence of who we've always been, and in our deepest nature still are: *we care. To be black means to care. About everything.* About orchids, and ancestors, about children and old people, about hair and history. It means accepting the pain and suffering of that condition, without drugs, or overeating, or sex addiction, or workaholism. It means trusting, as well, that the Universe will respond to our fidelity to our true nature by teaching us ways of being that will help us carry our unique burden—our deep, inevitable, irrevocable caring about people and the world—which is, at the same time, our most magnificent flower.

During my orchid "meditation," one orchid in particular, dewy dark blue, with a golden center, held my eyes. It was days before I realized that it reminded me of someone, my best friend, cousin and soulmate, when I was a child, whom everyone called Sister. We were like sisters growing up and wore identical dresses, snowsuits (though there was little snow in Georgia), white anklets and black patent-leather shoes. Grownups liked to call me cute, but to me Sister was the one. She was beautiful: glowing and dark like a peaceful night sky filled with bright stars. In fact the first time I saw a painting of the Goddess Nut, from inside an Egyptian pyramid, I had thought of her. The blue-black body of Nut, stretched across the sky, her milky way flowing toward all below, hungering, worshiping her, on earth. But the grownups did not consider Sister cute, let alone beautiful. In those days no African American person of any color was considered beautiful, and Sister was *black*; blackness itself was considered ugly. I thought the grownups were blind and crazy, but because I was a small child my view didn't count to them, nor did I have words to express it. I held tightly to Sister until she and her family moved north.

Sister eventually married someone who abused her. Later I would wonder about her self-esteem. How had she found a sense of herself as beautiful if no one around her could see it? I wished I had been there to whisper it in her ear every time she felt doubt. When I heard of her miserable life and even more miserable death, something inside almost lost hope that many black people can survive their own internalized self-hatred. How is it possible to hate the color black? What can we do to destroy the horrible prison of non-appreciation so many find themselves in? I began to think about blackness and what, over a lifetime, it still means to me.

Is American society and culture our rotten log? Our ordinary tree? Is America the burning house that James Baldwin thought we were integrating into? Can we learn how to live here? Can we thrive? If we cannot, perhaps we should not continue trying to live here. In fact, I have friends who are saying bittersweet good-byes, and leaving. They point to what is for them the final straw—

after the stolen election of 2000, the disen-
franchisement of black people, the growing sup-
pression of women's rights and burgeoning religious intolerance—the way that drug addiction is
changing even the character of humans; and drugs
are abundant in America. My friends feel life is too
short to try to blossom in soil soaked in poison. I
understand their position. However, if we can
learn how to blossom in our rotten log, our ordinary tree, or perhaps save enough of the burning
house to live in, in peace, how exactly do we ac-
complish that?

If you have ever seen happiness, you know what
it looks like. The experience of happiness is something one never forgets. What saves me from total
pessimism about our Being in America is that I
have experienced whole and healthy, mentally and
spiritually sound, deeply happy black people. But
they had obviously to learn how to live here. What
did these people have in common? A love of the
earth. A love of the sky above their heads. A love
of their fields and animals, if they were fortunate
enough to have them. A love of their neighbors
and compassion for the old and for children. A
reverence for growing things. An enjoyment of
life's daily miracles. A love of the Great Mystery.
And a deep and humble gratitude for having been
born in their perfectly wonderful bodies. They believed in community so much that they established
societies to look after "the sick and the shut-in"

and to make sure every person in the community had a decent burial. Homelessness and hunger were unheard of, for instance, in the community into which I was born. There were no orphans.

In meditation after yoga, consider the oneness of the planet, and how each part of it seems to have its own suffering. Wherever I have traveled I have found the same sorrows from different and sometimes the same mistakes; this makes me reluctant to abandon the country of my birth; many of its mistakes and sufferings I at least understand. I believe it is a time of great awakening, and that this awakening is global, hence the race by patriarchal powers worldwide to suppress and subjugate women, who, awake, are notorious for seeing why things are going wrong; and saying so.

Sit on the Earth, our Mother, and thank Her for her loyalty and devotion to you, whatever your condition or the condition of your people has been. Tell Her that wherever you go, you will never desert her. That you will do everything in your power to return to Her the care she has extended to you and yours. That you understand She is your true country and your eternal home. Kiss her pinecones, caress her turtle shells, admire the variety of her clouds, trees, oceans, beans. Remember, She is alive and wanting and needing affection, just as you do. You will be with Her always, though countries and governments crumble into Her dust.

Stretch out on Her breast, face to the grass. Allow your love, your pain, your confusion and sadness, your disappointment and hate, your fear, to fall into the only lap large enough to hold it all.

Look at that grass under your face, think of it as your own hair; what can you do to make it happier? And if you cannot imagine happy hair, or happy grass, how will you ever imagine happiness itself?

14.

To Be Led by Happiness
(Re: March 8, 2003)

I wrote this essay as a thank you to Medea Benjamin, an activist hero, who invited me to participate in this event and later asked if I would write an Op-Ed piece about it.

Not buying
War
Grief remains
Unsold.

It started with Einstein. I had written a poem about his hair. It wasn't just about his hair: I was thinking about his statement that World War III might be fought with nuclear weapons but World War IV would be fought with sticks and stones. I was walking down a gray, chilly street near my home in Berkeley, thinking about the sadness of his eyes, the sadness of our situation: about to invade and massively bomb Iraq, a country inhabited by old people, orphans, women and children. Boys

and men. The children, half the country's population, under fifteen years of age. I was thinking
about my impending journey to Washington,
D.C., to join a demonstration against the war; a
city whose streets, during slavery, were laid out
by Benjamin Bennaker, a free African American
(father African, mother Irish-African) tobacco
planter from Maryland. I thought of the ancestors
who, enslaved, built (eyes lowered, muscles strain-
ing), the imposing symbols of freedom in Washington, including the White House.

Though wanting to join the women of CODE
PINK who had been holding a vigil in front of the
White House for four months, dressed in pink to
signify the feminine concern for the safety, especially, of children, I was dreading the long lines at
the airport, and the flight. I stopped at a light,
thinking of how our experience now at airports,
being searched and sometimes seized, bears a re-
semblance worth scrutinizing to what Palestinians,
attempting to enter and leave their Israeli-
restricted areas, go through. Reflecting on this, I
rested my hand on a telephone pole before rather
wearily crossing the street. A piece of paper near
my hand fluttered in the wind. There, just above
my head, was another quote from Einstein someone had stapled to a pole. *The problems we face
today cannot be solved by the minds that created
them.*

It was a pretty grim message, perhaps grimmer
than the earlier one; still, I found myself beginning

to smile. Here he was: an ancestor who knew, and said out loud, that if we keep going in the direction we're headed, the jig is up. On the other side of the street I thought: Whose mind has not been heard at all on the direction we must immediately turn? The Mind of the Grandmothers of the World. But that's another story.

Ten thousand women dressed in hot pink, cool pink, all shades of pink, marched and rallied in Washington, D.C. to celebrate March 8, International Women's Day, 2003. There were rousing speeches; there was music and dance. Enormous and magical puppets. There was laughter and solemnity. The march was led by several rows of small children chanting "One Two Three Four, We Don't Want Your Crummy War: Five Six Seven Eight, We Will Not Participate." They were followed by writers and artists and activists, including Susan Griffin, Maxine Hong Kingston, Rachel Bagby, Terry Tempest Williams, Medea Benjamin, Nina Utne, and me. Behind us the sea of pink stretched far as the eye could see.

At Lafayette Park, across from the White House, we paused. Twenty-five of us were chosen to enter the park (a number previously authorized); only to find admittance denied. After a brief huddle, squatting at the knees of a line of police, we moved forward. Several hours later, having sung "Peace Salaam Shalom" and "Give Peace a Chance" the entire time, we were arrested. And it is of that moment, that hour—because it took a long time—that I wish to speak; and of our time in a holding cell before being set free.

I had been arrested before. While protesting apartheid in South Africa; while attempting to block the shipment of weapons, by train, to Central America. Those were serious times, but this time felt different. This time felt like: *All the information is in.* If our species does not outgrow its tendency to fight wars, we can kiss all we have created, and ourselves, good-bye. To bring children into the world at all, given the state of things, seems not only thoughtless but cruel. And it was of the children I thought, partly because there, right across from us, as we sang in front of the White House, were huge photographs of dismembered fetuses held by an anti-abortion group whose leader began to harangue us through a bullhorn. He called us traitors and murderers and accused us of nagging.

Nagging. What century was he from? we thought.

That he could not make the connection between the gruesomely dismembered bodies in his photographs and those of children bombed in Iraq seemed unbelievable. As he shouted at us we sang: "Protect the women and the children of Iraq." Eventually, scowling, looking extremely churlish, he left.

Standing between my Irish American sister

(Susan Griffin) and my Chinese American one (Maxine Hong Kingston), and with twenty-four other courageous women all around us; with Amy Goodman of *Democracy Now!* interviewing us for our communities across the world, and Kristin Michaels, a videographer, taping us, I felt the sweetest of all feelings: peace. The police began to gather their horses, their paddy wagons, their plastic handcuffs. We sang. Being women, we noticed and made much of the fact that a rainbow appeared suddenly in the sky.

Amy (who within minutes would be arrested herself) asked each of us how we felt about being arrested. Maxine said she felt it was the least she could do. I said I felt happier than I'd felt in years. Susan said her happiness went beyond happiness to joy. None of us could live with ourselves if we sat by and did nothing while a country filled with children, a lot of them disabled, homeless, and hungry, was blown to bits using money we need in the United States to build hospitals, housing and schools.

The arrest went smoothly. I thought the police were considerate, human. Some of us tried to help them do their job by sticking our arms out in front of us but the handcuffs go behind, not in front. We sang in the paddy wagons, we sang later in the holding cells. We recited poetry to each other and told stories from our lives. And all the while, there was this sweetness. Even though the floor of the cell, where some of us had to sit, was cold, and even though the toilet wouldn't flush. I found Fannie Lou Hamer's voice coming out of my throat and led our cell in singing "This Little Light of Mine."

I realized that, at the root of the peace cradling me, was not only Einstein, and other ancestors who told us the truth, but especially Martin Luther King, Jr. I had followed him faithfully since I was in my teens; his fearless, persistent struggle against injustice mesmerized me. *Perfect love casts out fear.* That is what he had. And that, ultimately, is what the sea of pink symbolized. We were women and children who loved ourselves in our Iraqi form of women and children; loving ourselves as humans meant loving ourselves as all humans. We understood that whatever we did to stop war, we did it not for the "other" but for a collective us. The heart enjoys experiencing the liberating feeling of compassion; it expands and glows, as if beaming its own sun upon the world. That is the warmth our cooling emotional world so desperately needs to preserve its humanity. It is this savoring of the ecstatic nature of impersonal love that lets the peacemakers of the world do our job. It is this love whose inevitable companion is not only peace, but happiness, and, as Susan said, joy.

We are the ones we have been waiting for.

Permissions

Grateful acknowledgment is made for permission to print or reprint the following material:

"Poem for South African Women" from *Passion: New Poems, 1977–80* by June Jordan. Copyright June Jordan; reprinted by permission of the June M. Jordan Literary Estate Trust (www.june jordan.com).

"Childhood" (chapter 2, this volume) by Alice Walker from *Dream Me Home Safely,* copyright 2003 by Children's Defense Fund. Published by Houghton Mifflin. Reprinted by permission of The Wendy Weil Agency, Inc.

"When Life Descends into the Pit" (poem near the start of chapter 3, this volume) from *By the Light of My Father's Smile* by Alice Walker, copyright 1998 by Alice Walker. Used by permission of Random House, Inc.

"A Blessing" by Stephen Philbrick. Used with permission of the author.

"Until I Was Nearly Fifty," "Loss of Vitality," "My Friend Yeshi," and "The Writer's Life" from *Absolute Trust in the Goodness of the Earth: New*